James Lawrence

Olde Englishe Recipes

Olde Englishe Recipes

Michelle Berriedale-Johnson

PIATKUS

© 1981 Michelle Berriedale-Johnson
First published in 1981 by Judy Piatkus (Publishers)
Limited of Loughton, Essex

Berriedale-Johnson, Michelle
   Olde Englishe Recipes.
   1. Cookery, English
   I. Title
   641.9542   TX717

   ISBN 0 86188 091 9

Line drawings by Paul Saunders

Typeset by Phoenix Photosetting, Chatham, Kent
Printed and bound by R. J. Acford, Chichester

Contents

Introduction

When one first comes across very old recipes, or 'receipts', in sixteenth-century manuals or early cookery books they tend to be rather unnerving. The profusion of ingredients and dearth of instructions quickly confuse the twentieth-century, cook, who is used to the ordered calm of a modern recipe book.

We should remember that our fifteenth- and sixteenth-century forefathers lived in less measured and regulated times. The nearest they came to having a controllable cooker was to draw a curtain around the open fire to regulate the draught. There were no weighing scales, and the books in which instructions would have been written were rare and precious and not to be trusted to the hustle and bustle of the kitchen.

This does not mean that there was no skill or art in their cookery; on the contrary. A great body of inherited knowledge and skills was passed from mother to daughter and from father to son. Sometimes this was written down in private manuals, which would include not only favourite recipes but also instructions for distilling and preserving, cures for the ague and septic cuts, tips on how to whiten stained linen and even recipes for getting rid of unwanted guests. Occasionally, as in the case of Anne Blencowe, these private collections were published.

The sixteenth and seventeenth centuries also saw the publication of manuals for the housewife, written by such men as Gervase Markham, Thomas Dawson and Sir Hugh Plat, which instructed the 'goodwife' in the countless duties involved in running her house and included recipes, simples and cures. What is more, most of the herbals and medical treatises which were published at that time, such as Andrew Boorde's *Dyetary* or *Breviary of Helthe*, contained advice on diet and frequent suggestions for its composition.

As the seventeenth century turned into the eighteenth, literacy spread among middle-class women and the printed word became more easily available. As a result, housewives' manuals written by women started to appear. Miss Smith, Mrs Glasse, Mrs Raffald and Mrs Rundell wrote books aimed at the growing numbers of city dwellers, the middle-class wives of successful merchants, shopkeepers and professional men. As Hannah Glasse says in her preamble:

'If I have not wrote in the high polite style I hope I shall be forgiven, for my intention is to instruct the lower sort and therefore must treat them in their own ways.'

In contrast, from about 1660 onwards there also appeared the works of professional cooks, for example Patrick Lamb, Robert May and William Gelleroy, all of whom published compendiums of the recipes they had used in the great houses where they had worked. Almost without exception, these men cooked in the French manner that had become popular after the Restoration of 1660, leaving the more homely English cooking to their female colleagues.

The nineteenth century saw a continuation of this trend. The professional cooks, Carême, Ude, Francatelli, Soyer, came from abroad and continued to cook in the French style; the ladies, culminating in Mrs Beeton and Mrs Marshall, wrote for the housewife.

It is from all these sources, the private manuals and the more formal cookery books of the eighteenth and nineteenth centuries, that I have drawn this collection of old English recipes.

I have selected recipes from as many periods and walks of life as possible. They have all been tested either at my home or in my catering company's kitchens. Some have been simplified and others adapted to make them more suitable for a modern kitchen, but I have always endeavoured to retain the original flavour of the dish. I have tried to give the derivation of each recipe whenever possible, and further information on many of the cooks, writers, gourmets and gourmands will be found at the end of the book.

I have cooked these dishes for many different people over the last year – English, American, European – and their reaction has always been the same: 'I never knew that old English food could taste so good!' I hope that you will agree.

MB-J

Pottages, Soups & Broths

BACON & HERB BROTH

A soup or pottage like this bacon and herb broth would have been a regular feature of a medieval peasant's day. Soups in the Middle Ages were known either as 'running' or 'standing' pottages; a running pottage, or broth, being a thin soup containing any bits of meat or vegetable that the housewife or cook had to hand. A standing pottage was thickened with breadcrumbs or rice until it was similar in consistency to a present-day mousse. For the peasant family the pottage normally 'ran' and its delectability would depend on the time of year and on what could be gathered from the hedgerows and forests. Hunks or 'sops' of bread would be thrown into the soup just before serving.

1 oz/25 g butter
4 oz/100 g bacon, diced
2 oz/50 g leeks, finely sliced
2 oz/50 g fennel, finely chopped
3 oz/75 g parsnips, diced
handful of parsley, chopped
bouquet garni
½ teaspoon black peppercorns
1½ pints/900 ml water
¼ medium-sized green cabbage, finely chopped
salt

Serves 8

Melt the butter in a pan and add the bacon, leek, fennel and parsnips. Fry gently for 5 minutes to soften the vegetables without colouring. Add the parsley, bouquet garni, peppercorns and water. Bring to the boil and simmer for 30 minutes. Add the cabbage and cook for another 5 minutes. Season to taste with salt and serve.

SAFFRON SOUP

Its bright yellow colour, slightly peppery taste and the fact that it actually grew in England (the town of Saffron Walden in Essex was one of the centres of its cultivation) made saffron a most popular spice in the Middle Ages.

To get a really medieval effect you could swirl a little parsley juice in the soup just before serving. This will give the soup a bright colour, and also make a pretty pattern!

1 lb/450 g onions, peeled and roughly chopped
2 cloves of garlic, peeled and roughly chopped
2 teaspoons powdered saffron
3 oz/75 g butter
2 oz/50 g wholemeal breadcrumbs
2 pints/1.2 litres chicken stock
5 fl oz/150 ml double cream
juice of 2 lemons
salt and pepper

Serves 8

Soften the onion, garlic and saffron in the butter. Add the breadcrumbs and chicken stock and simmer for 20 minutes. Liquidise or purée the soup. Add the cream and lemon juice and season to taste with salt and pepper.

The soup can be served either hot or cold.

ALMOND SOUP

Almonds, in all guises, were among the favourite foods of the noble classes during the Middle Ages – partly because they were flavoursome and highly nutritious, but also, no doubt, because they had to be imported at great expense from the Middle East! Like most Middle Eastern products (dried fruits, nuts and spices), they were almost unknown in England until after the First Crusade to the Holy Land at the beginning of the eleventh century.

1 clove, ½ blade of mace, 1 bay leaf and a sprig of basil
2 oz/50 g ham, diced
2 oz/50 g celery, diced
2 pints/1.2 litres chicken stock
8 oz/225 g ground almonds
2 fl oz/50 ml medium sherry
salt and white pepper
4 fl oz/100 ml double cream

Serves 8

Put all the herbs in a small muslin bag and place in a pan with the ham, celery and stock. Bring to the boil and simmer for 30 minutes. Add the almonds and simmer for another 15 minutes.

Remove the herb bag and purée the soup in a liquidiser or food processor. Add the sherry and cream and season to taste with salt and white pepper. Reheat to serve.

'TO MAKE A CULLIS AS WHITE AS SNOW' – Sir Hugh Plat

At the time Sir Hugh Plat published his Delights for Ladies *in 1609, a cullis was an essential ingredient in any dish that aspired to the high table. It was, in fact, a very rich stock derived from large quantities of meat boiled over a long period to extract all the goodness, after which the meat was discarded. As this seems an unnecessarily extravagant way of going about things, I have preserved the chicken and turned Sir Hugh's cullis into a soup.*

1 small boiling chicken
4 oz/100 g leeks, finely chopped
1 pint/600 ml white wine
1½ pints/900 ml water
juice of 1 lemon
bouquet garni
2 teaspoons ground ginger
1 oz/25 g castor sugar
10 fl oz/300 ml single cream
salt and white pepper

Serves 8

Put the chicken (whole) in a deep saucepan with the leeks, wine, water, lemon juice and bouquet garni. Bring to the boil and simmer gently for 1¼ hours.

Remove the chicken and take the flesh off the bones, keeping it in reasonably large pieces; return these to the soup. Make a paste with the ginger, sugar and a little cream and add to the soup. Add the rest of the cream and reheat gently.

Remove the bouquet garni and season to taste with salt and white pepper before serving.

ANNE BLENCOWE'S PEASE SOUPE

Thick, warming soups have always been popular in northern climes and England is no exception. Of the many thick soups that came out of English kitchens, green pea has always been a favourite, be it the split, dried pea soup of the Middle Ages or the puréed brew of the Victorian era (after which London's terrible smogs were named 'pea soupers').

Anne Blencowe's recipe dates from the seventeenth century and it is lighter in texture and flavour than many of its near relatives.

1 lb/450 g fresh or frozen green peas
1 leek, finely sliced
1 clove of garlic, crushed
1½ oz/40 g bacon, diced
3 oz/75 g butter
2 pints/1.2 litres ham stock
1 oz/25 g fresh spinach (if available)
1½ oz/40 g white cabbage, finely sliced
¼ lettuce, finely chopped
small handful of parsley, finely chopped
½ carton of mustard and cress
1 stalk celery, finely chopped
1 teaspoon dried mint
salt and pepper and a pinch of mace

Serves 6

Put the peas, leeks, garlic and diced bacon in a saucepan with half the butter. Fry gently until the vegetables are softened but not coloured. Add the stock. Bring to the boil and simmer for 20 minutes. Liquidise or purée in a food processor.

Meanwhile, melt the rest of the butter in another pan and sweat the spinach, cabbage, lettuce, parsley, celery, mustard and cress and the dried mint until soft.

Add the puréed peas to the sweated mixture. Season with salt, pepper and mace and reheat before serving.

POTAGE A LA REINE

Maybe it was after drinking a bowl of potage à la reine that Sydney Smith, the eighteenth-century parson and diarist, became convinced that 'character, talents, virtues and qualities are power-fully affected by beef, mutton, pie crust and rich soups.' For the soup would have served only as an accompaniment to the chicken and 'crusts well soaked' that were meant to fill the soup tureen.

A most modern way to serve the soup in 1759, but, I feel, a little too much for twentieth-century taste . . .

3 oz/75 g onions, chopped
3 oz/75 g carrots, diced
1 oz/25 g parsnip, diced
1 stalk of celery, chopped
2 parsley stalks
3 oz/75 g pie veal, diced
3 oz/75 g ham, diced
½ teaspoon salt
4 black peppercorns
pinch mace
2 slices white bread, with crusts removed
1¼ pints/750 ml water
1 oz/25 g ground almonds
yolk of 1 hard-boiled egg
2 fl oz/50 ml single cream
2 fl oz/50 ml medium sherry
2 oz/50 g cooked chicken, finely shredded

Serves 4

Put the onion, carrot, parsnip, celery, parsley stalks, veal, ham, salt, pepper, mace and bread in a saucepan with the water. Bring slowly to the boil and simmer for 1½ hours. Liquidise the soup and return it to the saucepan.

Mash the almonds with the egg yolk, add a little of the soup to make a paste and gradually add to the soup in the pan. Stir in the cream and sherry. Adjust the seasoning to taste and add the cooked chicken.

Reheat before serving.

SWEET MELON SOUP

Sweet fruit soups were very popular in the Middle Ages; there is one recipe for 'fyygge soupe' that consists almost entirely of puréed, dried fruits. The taste for sweet soups lasted until the nineteenth century, when Mrs Gaskell praised fellow diners who 'saw at a glance' that she liked sugar with her soup.

Melons were grown in England as early as the reign of James I; his apothecary, John Parkinson, gives directions in his herbal for their cultivation under glass, along with peaches, nectarines, oranges and lemons.

1 large ripe melon, cubed
1 oz/25 g butter
10 fl oz/300 ml milk
5 fl oz/150 ml single cream
5 fl oz/150 ml sweet white wine
2 teaspoons ground ginger
2 oz/50 g stem ginger
salt and white pepper

Serves 6

Lightly fry the melon cubes in the butter for 4 minutes. Add the milk, cream, white wine and ground ginger and bring to the boil. Simmer for 5 minutes, then purée in a liquidiser or food processor.

Slice the stem ginger thinly and add to the soup. Season to taste with salt and white pepper.

This soup can be served hot or cold, but the flavour comes through better if it is lightly chilled.

MOCK TURTLE SOUP

Turtle soup had, because of its rarity, become extremely fashionable by the end of the eighteenth century. Indeed, in the early 1800s a city banquet might well have featured no less than five different kinds of turtle soup – thick, thin, calipash, calipee and fin. However, such extravagance was far beyond the means of the average housewife so a substitute had to be found; a substitute that in due course became more popular than the original!

2 oz/50 g carrots, roughly chopped
2 oz/50 g celery, roughly chopped
2 oz/50 g onion, roughly chopped
juice and rind of ½ lemon
bouquet garni
6 black peppercorns
2 pints/1.2 litres clear beef stock
3 fl oz/75 ml Madeira or medium sherry
salt

Serves 4

Put the vegetables, lemon rind and juice, peppercorns and bouquet garni in a saucepan, add the stock and, *very* slowly, bring to the boil. Simmer for 30 minutes, allow to cool and leave to stand for 24 hours.

Strain the soup and discard the vegetables, rind, corns and bouquet garni. Add the Madeira or sherry, and season with salt to taste.

Reheat to serve but do not boil. Serve with cheese straws or biscuits.

MULLIGATAWNY

'Pepper water', it was called by Dr Kitchiner. He thought it 'a most fashionable soup and a great favourite with our East Indian friends.'

Although curries of various kinds made their way back to England from the mid 1700s onwards, most of what the English ate while in India remained totally chauvinistic in character despite its patent unsuitability to the climate. There were even English cookery manuals translated into Tamil for the use of the native cooks!

1 oz/25 g butter
1 small onion, peeled and finely chopped
1 small apple, peeled, cored and chopped
1 small carrot, peeled and diced
½ turnip, peeled and diced
1 stick celery, finely chopped
1 oz/25 g ham, chopped
1 sprig parsley
2 cloves, 1 bayleaf, ½ teaspoon thyme
½ dessertspoon curry powder
1 oz/25 g flour
½ dessertspoon curry paste
1½ pints/900 ml beef stock
5 fl oz/150 ml medium sherry
salt and pepper

Serves 6

Melt the butter in a saucepan and gently fry the onion, apple, carrot, turnip, celery, ham, herbs and spices for 5 minutes, stirring all the time to ensure they do not burn.

Mix together the curry powder and flour and then add the curry paste. Mix well, add to the vegetables and cook for a couple of minutes. Stir in the stock, bring to the boil and simmer for 30 minutes.

Remove the soup from the heat and purée it in a liquidiser or food processor.

Return the soup to the saucepan. Add the sherry and season to taste with salt and pepper. Reheat.

Traditionally, this soup is served with small pieces of cooked chicken floated in it and with a bowl of plain boiled rice as a side dish. Alternatively, serve with toast.

SAXE COBURG SOUP

The Victorians were never happy with a dish unless it 'had a name'.
Their cookery books are filled with exotic-sounding recipes based on
exceedingly prosaic ingredients – which is not to suggest that they
were any the worse for that! Presumably it was the same passion for
dissimulation that drove them to cover the indecent leg of a chair
with a skirt and to christen Brussels sprout soup Saxe Coburg!

1 oz/25 g butter
2 oz/50 g onion, chopped
1 oz/25 g bacon, diced
12 oz/350 g Brussels sprouts, cleaned and chopped
1 oz/25 g flour
1 teaspoon castor sugar
½ teaspoon each mace and black pepper
10 fl oz/300 ml milk
2 pints/1.2 litres ham stock
2 fl oz/50 ml dry white wine

Serves 6

Melt the butter in a saucepan and add the onion, bacon
and sprouts. Cover and cook gently for 15 minutes. Add
the flour, stir well and cook for a further 2 minutes. Add
the sugar, spices, milk, stock and wine, bring to the boil
and simmer for 15 minutes or until the sprouts are soft.
Purée the soup in a liquidiser or food processor.

Adjust the seasoning to taste (if the ham stock was salty
the soup will probably not need any additional salt) and
serve hot with plenty of croûtons.

Rere Supper Dishes, Light Luncheon Dishes & Hors d'oeuvres

RASTONS

Rastons were an ingenious medieval way of using up stale bread and varying the usual meat ration of bacon. For most people living on the land, pork and bacon were the only meats they would see from November to April — unless they managed to snare a rabbit or catch a pigeon. However, the penalties for poaching any game (the exclusive property of the king or overlord) were so fearsome that few would risk it.

6 large white or brown rolls
4 oz/100 g bacon, diced
5 oz/150 g butter
5 oz/150 g mushrooms, sliced
1 teaspoon each black pepper and cinnamon
2 oz/50 g raisins
4 oz/100 g cheese (optional)

Serves 6

Cut the tops off the bread rolls. Take most of the crumbs out of the inside of the rolls and from the tops and crumble it as much as possible. Fry the bacon and the crumbs in 4 oz/100 g of the butter until the crumbs begin to turn colour. Add the mushrooms and cook for a further couple of minutes. Add the seasoning and the raisins, mix well and pile into the rolls.

Dot the lids with the remaining butter and put them, plus the rolls, in a moderately hot oven (190°C/375°F/Gas Mark 5) for 10 minutes. Cover the rolls with the crisp lids and serve at once.

If you prefer a more savoury, twentieth-century flavour, leave out the raisins and grate the cheese over the top of the rolls. In this case, put the rolls under a hot grill for 5 minutes to melt and brown the cheese and serve the lids separately.

HERB & BACON PIE

This pie is another attempt to vary the working man's unchanging winter diet of salt pork or bacon and herbs.

In Langland's great fourteenth-century poem, Piers Plowman's lament shows all too clearly how the late-winter shortages could hit the peasant's family:

*I've no penny' quoth Piers, 'young pullets to buy —
And I say, by my soul, I have no salt bacon,
Only onion and parsley and cabbage like plants . . .
By such food must we live till Lammas time comes . . .*

1 lb/450 g lean bacon, thinly sliced
8 oz/225 g leeks, finely chopped
8 oz/225 g spinach, finely chopped
1 carton of mustard and cress
2 oz/50 g fresh watercress, chopped
large handful of parsley, finely chopped
leaves from 2 sprigs each fresh thyme and savory
2 sage leaves, chopped
3 eggs
5 fl oz/150 ml chicken stock
salt and pepper
8 oz/225 g shortcrust pastry

Serves 8

Remove the rinds from the bacon and fry the rashers in their own fat until crisp. Line an 8-inch/20-cm flan dish with half of the bacon. Mix the leeks, spinach, cresses and herbs and pile them on top.

Beat 2 of the eggs and add the stock. Season lightly with salt and pepper and pour over the vegetables. Lay the remaining bacon over the top and cover with pastry.

Decorate the pie with the pastry ends and brush with the remaining egg. Bake in a moderate oven (180°C/350°F/Gas Mark 4) for 40 minutes.

Serve warm.

HENRY IV'S SPICED CHICKEN MOUSSE

The original recipe for this dish, which was served at Henry IV's coronation in 1399, contained a far higher proportion of spices, fruits and seasonings than the one I give below. It would probably have been eaten as an accompaniment to a roast meat rather than as a dish on its own.

However, a guest at the coronation feast would, no doubt, have been far more interested in the entertainments going on around him than in the food! Processions of gifts, such as 'falcons and hunting dogs, silver vessels, armour and cloth of purple and gold', to be offered to the chief guest followed each course. Even the service of each dish, by a herald on horseback, could be quite entertaining! If all else failed, the jesters were on hand to provide amusement, and that could necessitate diving head first into a large bowl of custard!

6 spring onions, cleaned and finely chopped
½ tablespoon honey
5 fl oz/150 ml white wine
8 oz/225 g cooked chicken meat, minced
½ oz/15 g currants
pinch each of ground cloves and ginger
1 teaspoon salt
¼ teaspoon white pepper
¼ oz/10 g gelatine
juice of 1 orange
2 eggs, separated
3 fl oz/75 ml double cream

Serves 4

Put the onion, honey and wine in a saucepan, bring to the boil and simmer for 10 minutes. Put the chicken meat in a bowl with the currants, spices and seasonings. Add the honey and wine mixture and mix well.

Soften the gelatine in the orange juice and melt it over boiling water. Cool slightly and add to the mixture, along with the egg yolks. Lightly whisk the cream and fold in. Finally, whisk the egg whites until they just hold their shape, and fold them into the mousse.

Pour the mousse into a soufflé dish and chill for a few hours before serving.

GERVASE MARKHAM'S PAIN PERDY

Pain perdy is a prime example of how a successful dish will stand the test of time. Anyone acquainted with American breakfast menus will instantly recognise their favourite French toast lurking under the old French title of 'lost bread'.

1 large or 2 small spring onions, finely chopped
1 tablespoon parsley, chopped
3 oz/75 g butter
6 eggs
juice of 1 orange
salt and pepper
pinch each of ground cinnamon and nutmeg
4 thick slices crustless wholemeal bread
8 crisply fried slices bacon (optional)
honey or maple syrup (optional)

Serves 4

Fry the onion and parsley lightly in 1 oz/25 g of the butter until softened and lightly browned. Beat the eggs and add the orange juice, fried onion and parsley, salt, pepper and spices. Beat well together. Put the bread slices in a flat dish and pour over the egg mixture, allowing it to soak well into the bread.

Heat the rest of the butter in a large frying pan. Carefully lift the bread slices into the pan and pour any spare egg mixture left in the dish over the top. Fry briskly until the bread is puffed and browned (but not burnt) on the bottom. Turn carefully and fry the other side. Lift onto a warmed dish and serve at once with crisply fried bacon, honey or maple syrup.

ENGLISH RAREBIT

Over the centuries, cheese has not only provided the working man with his most reliable protein food but it has inspired more accolades than almost any other food. From Thomas Tusser:
  'Where fish is scant and fruit of trees,
  Supply that want with butter and cheese . . .'
From Brillat-Savarin:
  'A dessert without cheese is like a pretty woman with only one eye.'
And they would have both sympathised with Ben Gunn on his desert island:
  'Many a night I have dreamed of cheese — toasted mostly . . .'

2 oz/50 g butter
7 fl oz/200 ml real ale or beer
12 oz/350 g Cheddar, Lancashire or other strong English cheese, grated
1 teaspoon whole-grain English mustard
1 teaspoon Worcestershire sauce
celery salt
freshly ground black pepper
4 slices toasted wholemeal bread

Serves 4

Melt the butter and gradually add the beer and the cheese, stirring continually. Stir in the mustard, Worcestershire sauce and seasonings to taste. Put the toast in an ovenproof dish and spoon over the cheese mixture. Cook under a hot grill for 3 minutes or until the cheese is browned and bubbling.
  Serve at once with real ale to drink.

SPINACH FROISE

Eggs were particularly useful in the days before the instant heat of gas and electricity. They could be cooked on the embers of a dying fire, when it might have taken half an hour to get a solid fuel stove or an open fire hot enough to cook a piece of meat!

In Tudor times, when this omelette was invented, eggs were far smaller than they are today and it would have taken four eggs per person. A froise was the name normally given to an omelette filled with bacon, or, as in this case, with tongue; a tansy was one filled with herbs.

3 oz/75 g butter
3 oz/75 g cooked spinach, chopped
2 oz/50 g currants, washed
3 oz/75 g cooked tongue, chopped
½ teaspoon each salt and ground cinnamon
¼ teaspoon each ground mace, cloves and ginger
8 eggs
salt

Serves 6

Melt half the butter in a frying pan and add the spinach, currants, tongue and spices; stir well and warm through gently. In a bowl whisk the eggs lightly and season with the salt. Add the filling to the eggs.

Heat the remains of the butter in an omelette pan until sizzling and pour in the egg mixture. Cook quickly until browned on one side, turn and cook on the other side. Turn out onto a plate and serve either warm or cold.

JOAN CROMWELL'S ARTICHOKE PIE

When Charles II returned to the throne after the Puritan revolution of 1640–60, the royalists were interested in anything that might serve as propaganda to discredit the Cromwellian era. This was what they hoped to achieve (by showing what a mean, penny-pinching household Protector Cromwell had run) in publishing a book of household 'receipts' written by Oliver Cromwell's wife, Joan. Unfortunately for the royalists, the plan completely backfired as the book, with its many practical and excellent recipes, became an instant best seller!

8 oz/225 g shortcrust pastry
4 oz/100 g bacon, thinly sliced and chopped
6 artichoke hearts, cooked (canned or frozen will do)
1 oz/25 g raisins
2 oz/50 g dates, stoned and roughly chopped
¼ teaspoon each ground ginger and mace
1 egg
2 fl oz/50 ml sweet sherry
grated rind and juice of 1 orange
1 teaspoon dark brown sugar

Serves 6

Roll out two-thirds of the pastry and line an 8-inch/20-cm flan dish; bake it blind.

Lightly fry the bacon in its own fat. Fill the flan dish with the bacon, artichoke hearts, and the raisins and dates mixed with the spices.

Cover with the rest of the pastry and decorate, leaving a small hole in the lid. Brush with beaten egg. Cook for 20 minutes in a moderately hot oven (190°C/375°F/Gas Mark 5).

Heat the sherry, orange juice and rind with the sugar and pour through the hole in the crust. Return to the oven for a further 10 minutes at a lower heat (180°C/350°F/Gas Mark 4), or until the pastry is cooked.

SEVENTEENTH-CENTURY BROAD BEAN TART

The original recipe for this tart, which dates from 1695, tells the reader to layer the beans with 'wet sweetmeats as of Apples, Apricocks, Peaches, Pears, Plums etc and between each layer to strew a little sugar.' It then goes on to season the mixture with 'salt, Cloves, mace, Nutmegs, and Candid Limon and Orange Peel.'

I feel that this combination is a little too sweet for today's palate and I have reduced the spices and added a little ham; the result is quite delicious.

    8 oz/225 g wholemeal, shortcrust pastry
    4 oz/100 g tart eating apples, peeled and diced
    8 oz/225 g fresh or frozen broad beans
    4 oz/100 g ham, diced
    3 eggs
    1 teaspoon whole-grain mustard
    ½ teaspoon dark brown sugar
    salt and pepper
    10 fl oz/300 ml cider

Serves 8

Roll out the pastry and line an 8-inch/20-cm flan case; bake it blind.

Cook the beans in boiling, slightly salted water until they are just tender. In a bowl, beat the eggs with the mustard, sugar and seasoning. Add the beans, diced apple and ham and mix together. Add the cider and beat well. Pour into the flan case and cook in a slow oven (150°C/300°F/Gas Mark 2) for approximately 50 minutes or until the custard is set.

Serve warm or cold.

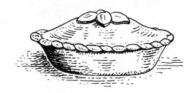

'BOYLED GARLIK'

Andrew Boorde's rather bizarre comment that 'garlyke, of all rootes, is used and most prised in Lombardy for it doth open the breste' is explained by the apparently successful herbal remedy for bronchitis which required one to make a syrup of garlic boiled in honey. John Evelyn, however, found garlic 'intolerably rank – not fit for ladies' palates, or those who court them.'

Despite its strength when raw, garlic does lose its rankness in the cooking and if one survives the smelly and fiddly job of peeling the cloves, the result is delicate and unusual.

2 oz/50 g butter
pinch each of saffron, mace and salt
½ teaspoon cinnamon
15 fl oz/450 ml water
cloves from 12 bulbs of garlic, peeled
4 slices toasted wholemeal bread, buttered

Serves 4

Put the butter and spices in a small saucepan, add the water and bring to the boil. Add the garlic cloves and simmer for approximately 7 minutes or until the garlic is easily pierced with a fork. Drain.

Serve the garlic on freshly toasted and buttered bread.

JOHN FARLEY'S PICKLED MACKEREL

'Mistress, it were good to remember your stock of herring now this fishing time for you shall do more now with forty shillings than you will at Christmas with five marks (about sixty six shillings).' So wrote her bailiff to Margaret Paston in 1479. The same principle applied three centuries later: John Farley always pickled his mackerel when it was cheap and plentiful against the time when stocks should run low.

The strength of the pickle has been reduced slightly in this recipe as the twentieth-century cook will tend to keep fish in a refrigerator or freezer, but pickled mackerel still makes a very tasty snack with plenty of brown bread and butter or wholemeal toast.

2 teaspoons fine sea salt
1 teaspoon freshly ground black pepper
2 teaspoons freshly ground nutmeg
1 teaspoon ground mace
4 mackerel, cleaned and cut into 1½-inch/3-cm slices
corn or sunflower oil
3 tablespoons olive oil
1 tablespoon wine vinegar

Serves 6

Mix the salt and spices together and rub them well into the slices of fish, making occasional little cuts in the flesh of the fish to enable the spices to permeate further. Cover and leave on one side for a couple of hours.

Heat the corn or sunflower oil in a frying pan, and gently fry the mackerel pieces until they are browned all over and cooked through – this should take about 4 minutes, depending on the size of the mackerel. Remove from the pan and cool.

To serve, put the mackerel pieces in a dish and pour over a dressing made of the olive oil and vinegar, which have been thoroughly mixed together.

WILLIAM VERRAL'S ANCHOVIES WITH CHEESE

'This seems but a trifling thing,' says William Verral in his Cook's Paradise, *'but I never saw it come whole from the table.' Anchovies were greatly used in the seventeenth and eighteenth centuries as a 'whip and spur' to a flagging thirst during an evening's carousing!*

    8 fingers of wholemeal bread
    8 anchovy fillets
    3 tablespoons of oil from the anchovies, or butter
    2 oz/50 g well-flavoured cheese
    freshly ground black pepper
    juice of 1 orange

Serves 4

Fry the bread fingers lightly on both sides in the oil or butter. Place one anchovy fillet on each finger, put them on an ovenproof serving dish and grate over the cheese. Place under a hot grill for about 3 minutes to melt and brown the cheese. Grind over some black pepper and sprinkle with the orange juice. Serve at once.

    This dish is equally good as a savoury or cocktail snack.

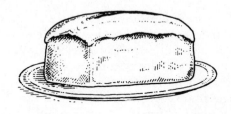

WILLIAM VERRAL'S 'MACAROONS' WITH CHEESE

'These are to be had,' says William Verral in his recipe, referring to the 'macaroons', 'at any confectioner's shop in London and the newer they are the better. But this is not what we call macaroons of the sweet biscuit sort, but a foreign paste the same as Vermicelli, but made very large in comparison to that.'

Of course, what he is actually talking about is macaroni . . .

8 oz/225 g fresh or dried 'large' pasta
1 oz/25 g butter
8 spring onions, chopped
handful of parsley, chopped
4 oz/100 g cockles, clams, prawns, shrimps, mussels or scallops, cooked
5 fl oz/150 ml double cream
2 fl oz/50 ml dry white wine
salt and pepper
2 oz/50 g ricotta or mozzarella cheese

Serves 4

Cook the pasta in boiling salted water until it is just cooked but still 'al dente' – approximately 5 minutes for fresh and 12–15 minutes for dried. Drain and rinse in boiling water.

Melt the butter in a pan and gently fry the onions for 3 minutes. Add the parsley, fish, cream and wine and cook for a couple of minutes. Season well.

Mix the pasta with the sauce and turn into a heated ovenproof dish. Crumble cheese over the top and bake in a hot oven (200°C/400°F/Gas Mark 6) for 15 minutes. Grind some pepper over the top and serve immediately.

EGGS AU MIROIR

William Verral gives this recipe for eggs in cream along with another called 'eggs au soleil', which involves deep frying poached eggs in an ale batter.

It is a little difficult to see where the mirror comes into it, but this recipe has what John Evelyn would have called a 'grateful gust', thanks to the orange and lemon juice.

> 3 good white rolls
> 6 eggs
> 12 spring onions, finely chopped
> 2 handfuls of parsley, finely chopped
> 1 oz/25 g butter
> juice of 1 orange and 1 lemon
> salt, pepper and a pinch of nutmeg
> 8 fl oz/225 ml double cream

Serves 6

Halve the rolls and remove most of the crumbs from the centres. Arrange the rolls either in one large dish or in individual ramekin dishes. Break one egg into each roll. Gently fry the onions and parsley in the butter until soft. Add the orange and lemon juice, the seasoning and the cream. Mix well and spoon over the eggs.

Bake in a moderate oven (160°C/325°F/Gas Mark 3) for 9 minutes or until the egg whites are just set.

Serve at once.

LETTUCE STUFFED WITH FORCEMEAT

In the sixteenth and seventeenth centuries even lettuce, the mildest of vegetables, was thought 'flatulent and indigestible' if eaten raw. So, as with all other vegetables, cooking was recommended if one wished to avoid consulting Robert Burton's list of 57 herbs guaranteed to relieve 'windiness'!

4 small cabbage lettuces
$\frac{1}{2}$ oz/15 g bacon fat
1 medium-sized onion, finely chopped
4 oz/100 g bacon, diced
4 oz/100 g brown breadcrumbs
pinch of thyme
$\frac{1}{2}$ teaspoon nutmeg
1 egg
juice of 1 orange
salt and pepper
4 spring onions, chopped
7 fl oz/200 ml chicken stock
3 fl oz/75 ml medium sherry

Serves 4

Wash the lettuces without dismembering them. Melt the bacon fat and fry the onion and bacon until lightly browned. Put the breadcrumbs, thyme, nutmeg, egg and orange juice in a bowl and mix well; add the onion and bacon and season to taste.

Gently pull the lettuces apart and stuff the centre of each with a quarter of the mixture. Put the lettuces in a casserole or pie dish just large enough to hold them, sprinkle over the spring onions and pour over the stock and sherry.

Cover and cook in a moderate oven (180°C/350°F/Gas Mark 4) for 30 minutes. Serve at once with the juice.

SALAMAGUNDY

A salamagundy was a cold platter, very popular in the eighteenth century, made up of a selection of small dishes, not unlike a modern hors d'oeuvre. The essence of the dish was that it should combine very bland with very spicy flavours. As long as this contrast was achieved almost any ingredients could be used.

The various elements should be arranged on a round table if possible, forming a pyramid with the central dishes standing above the outlying ones. The gaps between the little bowls or dishes should be filled with fresh, edible flowers and herbs, such as nasturtiums, marigolds, parsley, sage, watercress and so on. These are some examples of foods that could be used:

Bland foods:
    hard-boiled eggs, yolks and whites in separate dishes
    cooked chicken meat
    mayonnaise
    cold roast pork
    chopped celery
    soft cream cheese
    cooked white fish
    cooked rice
    cucumbers
    raw mushrooms

Spicy foods:
    sharp oil and vinegar dressing
    pickled walnuts and onions
    sharp chutneys or made up pickles
    sliced raw onions
    anchovies
    pickled mackerel or herring
    radishes
    sliced red cabbage
    gherkins or dill cucumbers

HOT CHEESE LOAF

Stale bread always had a use in an English kitchen! In medieval times 'trencher' bread, which served many people as a plate, had to be four days old in order to soak up the gravy properly; while a loaf baked on Good Friday was hung in the kitchen to ward off evil spirits. In later centuries a loaf would be left hanging so that the mould (full of penicillin) could be used for treating gunshot wounds.

In this recipe, old, rather dry, bread will soak up the wine admirably to make a base for the pasta.

1 small stale loaf of brown or white bread
10 fl oz/300 ml white wine
1 oz/25 g butter
6 spring onions, chopped
½ oz/15 g cornflour
15 fl oz/450 ml milk
5 fl oz/150 ml single cream
6 oz/175 g Cheshire, Lancashire or strong English cheese
salt, pepper and nutmeg to taste
8 oz/225 g cooked pasta, any shape

Serves 6

Halve the loaf and put it in the bottom of a flan dish, crust downwards. Pour over the wine, cover and set aside for 30 minutes.

Melt the butter in a saucepan. Gently cook the spring onions in the butter, then add the cornflour and cook for a couple of minutes before gradually adding the milk and cream. Cook for several minutes, stirring continually, until the sauce thickens.

Add 4 oz/100 g of the cheese and salt, pepper and nutmeg to taste. Stir in the pasta, mix well and spoon over the loaf in the dish. Sprinkle over the remaining cheese and put under a hot grill for approximately 5 minutes or until the cheese is well browned and the bread is heated through. Serve.

ROYAL MACARONI

This simple but rich dish would have appealed to Queen Victoria in her later years when she had turned away from the elaborate meals of eight to ten courses prepared for her by Francatelli in the 1840s. It is said that at the end of her life she would often dine on a single boiled egg served in a golden cup, attended only by her Scottish gamekeeper and an Indian boy.

> 1 lb/450 g macaroni
> 12 fl oz/350 ml double cream
> 2 oz/50 g butter
> 10 oz/250 g white Stilton or Lancashire cheese
> salt, pepper, mace, nutmeg and cayenne
> 2 oz/50 g toasted brown breadcrumbs

Serves 4

Cook the macaroni in fast boiling water for 10 minutes or until it is cooked but still 'al dente'.

Heat the cream in a saucepan and gradually add the butter and cheese, stirring continually. Season with salt, pepper, cayenne, nutmeg and mace to taste. Add the cooked macaroni and reheat in the sauce. Turn into a warmed serving dish, sprinkle with the toasted bread-crumbs and serve at once.

BAKED EGGS WITH TOMATOES

For this recipe, as for all baked egg recipes, the flavour is improved if the eggs are absolutely fresh. Mrs Rundell, the author of the nineteenth-century book Domestic cookery by a Lady, *gives the following advice: 'To choose eggs at market. Put the large end of the egg to your tongue — if it feels warm it is new. In new laid eggs there is a small division of the skin from the shell which is filled with air and is perceptible to the eye at the end. On looking through them against the sun or a candle, if fresh they will be pretty clear. If they shake they are not fresh.'*

6 slices wholemeal bread
4 oz/100 g butter
6 slices tomato
3 oz/75 g onions, finely chopped
3 oz/75 g mushrooms
4 fl oz/100 ml sour cream
salt and pepper
6 large eggs

Serves 6

Cut a hole in the middle of each piece of bread large enough to hold one slice of tomato. Fry the bread slices until crisp in 3 oz/75 g of the butter. Set out on a flat ovenproof dish and fill each hole with a slice of tomato.

Melt the remaining butter in a pan and gently cook the onions and mushrooms until soft. Add the cream and seasoning and mix well.

Break one egg over each slice of tomato and spoon over the mushroom mixture to cover the egg, if possible. Cook in a moderate oven (160°C/325°F/Gas Mark 3) for 15 minutes or until the egg whites are set.

Fishes ~ salt & sweet, devilled & forced

MUSSEL & FENNEL STEW WITH DUMPLINGS

We know that oysters and mussels were on English menus as early as 200 BC, for their shells have been found in various Roman settlements. People living near the sea therefore, in medieval times, might well have cheered up the Friday fast day by stewing some mussels with the fennel roots that would have grown in the garden.

2 oz/50 g butter
1 oz/25 g bacon, diced
4 oz/100 g leeks, finely sliced
1 head fennel, finely chopped
juice of 1 lemon
12 fl oz/350 ml dry white wine
12 fl oz/350 ml water
salt and pepper
pinch of mace
2 lb/900 g fresh mussels in their shells or 10 oz/275 g frozen
    mussels
10 fl oz/300 ml single cream

Dumplings:
2 oz/50 g leeks, finely chopped
1 oz/25 g butter
1 tablespoon parsley, finely chopped
3 oz/75 g brown breadcrumbs
2 tablespoons water
1 egg
salt and pepper
pinch of mace

Serves 4

In a deep pot, melt the butter and add the bacon, leek and fennel and fry gently until soft. Add the lemon juice, wine, water, a little salt and pepper and the mace.

If the mussels are fresh, wash them well to ensure they are all good (if any one fails to close when soaked in fresh water it means that it is dead and should be discarded) and add them to the stew in their shells. If the mussels are frozen, just add them to the pot. Bring to the boil and simmer for 5 minutes to ensure that the mussels are cooked. Add the cream and adjust the seasoning.

To make the dumplings, gently fry the leek in the butter until soft. Add the breadcrumbs, parsley, water, egg and seasoning and mix well together. Form into small balls and chill.

Just before serving bring the stew to the boil and drop in the dumplings. Boil for 3 minutes to cook the dumplings and serve at once.

STRIPED FISH PIE

The black and white stripes of this pie would have delighted a medieval chef, who liked nothing better than to make dramatic and eye-catching patterns with food. The fruits that it contains in such quantities were expensive and rare, and would have had the added advantage, in his eyes, that their strong flavours would help hide the ever-present flavour of the salt fish he normally used.

1 lb/450 g shortcrust pastry
8 oz/225 g raisins
8 oz/225 g currants
4 oz/100 g prunes, stoned
4 oz/100 g figs, dried
2 teaspoons ground ginger
2 lb/900 g cooked white fish – haddock or cod for preference
salt and pepper
2 oz/50 g whole almonds
4 fl oz/100 ml fish stock or fish stock mixed with white wine
1 egg

Serves 8

Line a loose-bottomed cake tin (approximately 7 in/ 18 cm in diameter) with two-thirds of the pastry.

Reserve 1 oz/25 g of the currants. Chop the prunes, figs and raisins finely (this can be done in a food processor) and mix them with the rest of the currants and the ginger.

Flake the fish and mix the reserved currants into it. Season with salt and pepper.

Put half the fruit mixture in the bottom of the lined cake tin and flatten out. Cover this with the fish and currant mixture. Mix the whole almonds into the rest of the fruit mixture and pile it into the pie. Pour over the fish stock or stock and wine.

Cover the pie with the remaining pastry, using the scraps to decorate the lid with little fish. Beat the egg and brush the pie with it. Cook in the centre of a moderate oven (180°C/350°F/Gas Mark 4) for 25–30 minutes or until the pastry is cooked.

Serve warm or cold with a good sharp salad.

FRESH WATER FISH BOILED
WITH HERBS

In the original version of this recipe, Sir Hugh Plat suggests that a 'pickerel' or young pike is used. However, one is unlikely to come across pike these days; because of their omniverous nature they have been, wherever possible, banned from British rivers and fish ponds. To quote Izaak Walton, 'All pikes that live long, prove chargeable to their keepers because their life is maintained by the death of so many other fish . . . which has made him be called by some writers, the tyrant of the rivers or the fresh water wolf.'

4 sprigs each of fresh thyme, mint, rosemary, watercress and parsley
1 medium-sized onion, sliced
½ lemon, sliced
2 oz/50 g butter
approximately 2 lb/900 g fresh water fish such as bream, carp, grayling, perch, pike or river trout, cleaned and filleted (or unfilleted if you prefer your fish whole)
1 teaspoon salt
8 black peppercorns
10 fl oz/300 ml dry white wine
10 fl oz/300 ml water
1 orange, sliced

Serves 4

Put the herbs, onion, lemon and butter in the bottom of a large frying pan. Lay the fish on top and sprinkle with salt and peppercorns. Pour over the wine and water. Bring to the boil and simmer, covered, for approximately 15 minutes or until the fish flakes easily and is cooked – the length of time will depend on the size and type of fish.

Remove the fish to a warmed serving dish, decorate with orange slices and serve immediately with fresh brown bread and butter.

MRS BLENCOWE'S OYSTER OR MUSSEL PIE

In 1694 when Mrs Blencowe was setting down her 'receipt', oysters were cheap and plentiful, and larger than those found today. Some were large enough to cut into eight pieces. In the eighteenth century Dr Johnson was even feeding them to his cat, Hodge!

If you can afford oysters, certainly use them; if not, mussels, the 'poor man's oysters', will do just as well.

4 oz/100 g brown breadcrumbs
2 teaspoons parsley, chopped
6 spring onions, finely chopped
3 oz/75 g anchovy fillets, chopped
1 lb/450 g shelled, cooked oysters or mussels – frozen mussels will do very well
freshly ground black pepper
8 oz/225 g shortcrust pastry
1 egg
2 small oranges

Serves 4

In a bowl mix together the breadcrumbs, parsley and spring onions. Add the anchovies and mussels or oysters, mix together and season with black pepper.

Line a pie dish with two-thirds of the pastry. Pile the fish mixture into the pie, top with the remaining pastry and decorate, leaving a small hole in the middle.

Beat the egg and brush the top of the pie. Add the orange juice to the remains of the egg and pour into the pie through the hole in the crust.

Bake in a moderate oven (180°C/350°F/Gas Mark 4) for 25 minutes or until the pastry is cooked and golden.

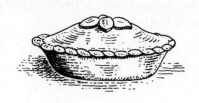

ROBERT MAY'S FISH PIE

Robert May was one of the first professional cooks not only to commit his recipes to paper but to publish them. His Accomplisht Cook *appeared in 1671 and includes, apart from complex and costly dishes for the nobility, many simpler recipes, like this fish pie, for 'those whose purses cannot reach to the Cost of Rich Dishes.'*

12 oz/350 g shortcrust pastry
12 oz/350 g white fish (plaice, sole, cod or haddock), boned and skinned
10 fl oz/300 ml white wine
½ lemon sliced
6 oz/175 g jellied eel, boned and roughly chopped
3 artichoke hearts, roughly chopped
3 oz/75 g gooseberries, fresh or frozen (unsweetened)
3 egg yolks plus 1 whole egg
juice of 1 small orange and ½ lemon
½ teaspoon salt
¼ teaspoon black pepper
½ teaspoon nutmeg
1 oz/25 g butter

Serves 6

Line an 8-inch/20-cm flan dish with two-thirds of the pastry and bake it blind.

Simmer the fish in the wine with the lemon slices for 10 minutes or until just cooked (the length of time it takes will depend on the size and type of fish used). Drain and flake the fish, reserving the wine-stock.

Arrange the white fish, jellied eel, artichoke hearts and gooseberries in the dish. Beat the egg yolks and add the reserved stock, orange and lemon juice and seasoning. Pour over the fish and dot with the butter.

Cover with the remaining pastry and decorate with pastry fishes etc. Brush with beaten egg and bake in a moderately hot oven (190°C/375°F/Gas Mark 5) for 25 minutes or until the pastry is nicely browned.

COLD STUFFED TROUT

'This kind of fish,' says Izaak Walton in his Compleat Angler, *'if he is not eaten within four or five hours after he is taken, is worth nothing.' The instant freezing techniques of the twentieth century guarantee total freshness, but in Walton's time half a day's journey in the sun could wreak havoc with a newly-caught trout.*

1½ oz/40 g butter
1 oz/25 g fat bacon, chopped small
4 spring onions, chopped
2 sprigs parsley, chopped
4 oz/100 g cod or other white fish
1 egg yolk, beaten
4 trout, gutted and boned but with the skin along the back whole
    and the head and tail left on
4 fl oz/100 ml double cream
juice of 1 orange and 4 slices of orange
salt and white pepper

Serves 4

In ½ oz/15 g of the butter gently fry the bacon and onion until soft but not coloured. Mash the cod with the parsley, add the onion and bacon, a little seasoning and the egg yolk. Mix well together and stuff each trout.

Place the stuffed trout in a buttered baking dish, dot with the remaining butter, cover and cook for 30 minutes in a moderate oven (180°C/350°F/Gas Mark 4), or for slightly longer if the fish are large. Remove from the oven and skin the fish carefully. Place them in a serving dish.

In a saucepan bring the cream to the boil. Add the orange juice, cook for a couple of minutes and season to taste. Pour the sauce over the trout and decorate each with an orange twist.

Serve cold but not chilled.

MACKEREL WITH FINE HERBS

'The first skill in cooking,' says Gervase Markham in his book,
English Huswife, *published in 1649, 'is to have a knowledge of
all sorts of Herbes belonging to the Kitchen, whether they be for the
Pot, for Sallets, for Sauces or for any other seasoning or adorning.'*
  *Certainly, this held true nearly two centuries later when William
Verral was devising his recipe for mackerel with 'fine herbs'.
Despite the variety, the flavours of the herbs do not clash but meld
with that of the mackerel to give freshness to the rich flesh of the fish.*

  2 large mackerel
  2 oz/50 g butter
  1 oz/25 g fennel, finely chopped
  2 spring onions, chopped small
  handful of parsley, finely chopped
  4 sprigs of thyme, fresh if possible
  2 small sage leaves, chopped small
  4 mint leaves, fresh if possible, chopped small
  a few rosemary leaves, chopped
  salt, pepper and a pinch of ginger
Sauce:
  4 spring onions, chopped
  1 oz/25 g butter
  juice of 1 orange
  2 soup ladles of good, light stock

Serves 4

Clean the mackerel, cut them open, bone them and divide
each into two fillets. Lay the fillets, skin downwards, in a
flat ovenproof dish.

  Soften the butter, then add the fennel, spring onion,
herbs, ginger and seasoning; beat into a paste and spread
this over the mackerel. Place under a hot grill for 5–10
minutes (depending on the size of the fish) until the mackerel are cooked.

  Meanwhile, for the sauce, soften the spring onion in the
butter. Add the orange juice and stock and boil briskly
together for a couple of minutes.

  Pour the sauce over the fish just before serving.

'SALMON IN SLICES WITH PRAWNS OR SHRIMPS'

In 1594, it was estimated by the cartographer, John Norden, that over 40,000 people lived off the fish that were caught every day in the Thames. Even as late as the 1830s it was possible to catch salmon in the Thames as well as flounder, smelt, eel, roach, lamprey and whitebait, but as Thomas Peacock makes clear in his novel, Crotchett Castle, *such a catch was quite an event!*

'Rarity of rarities – a Thames salmon, caught this morning . . . Indeed Sir, a Thames salmon has two virtues over all other; first that it is fresh and second that it is rare. For in some years, Sir, we catch not one! Mud, filth, gas dregs, lock weirs and the march of mind, developed in the form of poaching, have ruined the fishery. But when we do catch a salmon, happy the man to whom he falls!'

    1½ oz/40 g bacon fat
    6 spring onions, finely chopped
    3 oz/75 g mushrooms, chopped
    3 sprigs of parsley, finely chopped
    juice of 1½ lemons
    6 salmon steaks
    pepper and salt
Sauce:
    6 oz/175 g cooked shrimps (in their shells) or prawns
    2 anchovy fillets, chopped
    juice of 1 lemon
    4 spring onions, chopped
    2 mushrooms, sliced
    4 black peppercorns
    a few parsley stalks
    10 fl oz/300 ml dry white wine
    10 fl oz/300 ml water
    ½ oz/15 g flour
    juice of 2 oranges
    4 fl oz/100 ml single cream

Serves 6

Melt the bacon fat in a large frying pan and add the spring onion and chopped mushroom. Fry gently for a couple of minutes. Add the chopped parsley, lemon juice and a little seasoning and stir well. Lay the salmon steaks in the pan on the mirepoix of vegetables and spoon any excess over the top. Remove from the heat, cover and leave for 1 hour.

Transfer the steaks to a grill pan with the mirepoix and cook under a hot grill for 3–5 minutes, depending on the thickness of the steaks. Turn, keeping as much of the vegetable as possible stuck to the steaks, and cook for another couple of minutes. Remove to a heated serving dish and keep warm.

To make the sauce, put 4 oz/100 g of the shrimps or prawns into a saucepan with the anchovy, lemon juice, spring onion, mushroom, peppercorns, parsley stalks, wine and water. Bring to the boil and simmer for 15 minutes. Liquidise the sauce or put it through a food processor.

Meanwhile, mix the flour with the orange juice to make a smooth paste. Add the cream and add the whole mixture to the liquidised sauce.

Reheat and serve with the fish, which should be decorated with the remaining shrimps or prawns.

FILLETS OF SOLE WITH SPINACH

In the days of sail it was thought unlucky and ill-mannered to turn a sole over after eating the first side; to do so could augur the capsize of a ship. Instead, the bones were carefully peeled off and put on a side plate. History does not reveal what one was supposed to do if the fish had been filleted!

Spinach has always been a popular vegetable. John Evelyn was a great believer in its medicinal properties: 'A most excellent condiment with butter or vinegar; most profitable for the aged.'

1 oz/25 g butter
6 spring onions, chopped
2 oz/50 g bacon, chopped very small
2 oz/50 g ground almonds
2 oz/50 g brown breadcrumbs
¼ teaspoon each ground nutmeg and white pepper
1 teaspoon sea salt
12 oz/350 g fresh (cooked and chopped) or frozen (chopped)
   spinach
juice of ½ orange and ½ lemon
1 egg
6 large fillets of lemon sole
10 fl oz/300 ml good fish stock made from the bones and skin of
   the fish. If this is not available use half water and half dry
   white wine.
½ oz/15 g flour
5 fl oz/150 ml double cream
½ teaspoon dill weed
salt and pepper

Serves 6

Melt ½ oz/15 g of the butter in a pan and gently fry the spring onion and bacon until they are soft but not coloured. Turn into a bowl and add the almonds, breadcrumbs, spices and seasoning. Stir in the spinach and the fruit juices. Beat the egg and add to the mixture.

Lay the fillets out on a board and divide the mixture between them. Roll them up *loosely* and place in a baking tin. Pour over the fish stock.

Cover the tin with foil and cook in a moderate oven (180°C/350°F/Gas Mark 4) for 30 minutes. Cool in the liquid. Transfer the fillets to a serving dish and reserve the fish stock.

Melt the remaining butter in a pan, add the flour and cook for a couple of minutes. Gradually add the liquid from the fish, the cream and dill weed. Cook for a couple of minutes, and adjust the seasoning to taste.

Meanwhile, reheat the fish and pour the sauce over immediately before serving.

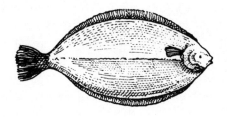

MRS RAFFALD'S RAISED SALMON PIE

One sixteenth-century suggestion for catching salmon is to 'go to the pool where the salmon lies and make a little hole hard by the waterside and set in your candle and take a brightly scoured basin and set it behind the candle and it will come to the candle as if by nature.' Would that it were so simple!

Mrs Raffald raises her pie around a pie-mould 'putting flowers and leaves on the walls'. We take an easier way.

Pastry:
  1 lb/450 g plain flour
  salt
  ½ teaspoon icing sugar
  4 oz/100 g lard
  7 fl oz/200 ml water

Filling:
  2 oz/50 g butter
  8 oz/225 g onions, finely chopped
  1 lb/450 g mushrooms, wiped and sliced
  2 handfuls of parsley, chopped
  2 lb/900 g cooked salmon
  ½ teaspoon salt
  ¼ teaspoon black pepper
  ½ teaspoon each ground mace and nutmeg
  ½ oz/15 g anchovy fillets
  1 egg

Serves 8

Sift the flour, salt and icing sugar into a bowl and make a hollow in the middle. Heat the fat in the water until the former has melted and the latter is boiling. Pour it into the well in the flour, stirring continuously with a wooden spoon to draw in all the flour. Knead with your hand until the paste forms a compact ball. Cover with a cloth and leave to cool slightly.

Melt 1 oz/25 g of the butter in a frying pan and add the onion. Cook until the onion begins to soften, then add the mushrooms and parsley and cook for a further minute.

Mash the salmon and season with the salt, pepper and ground mace and nutmeg.

Take two-thirds of the pastry and with your fingers press it over the base and up the sides of a loose-bottomed 7-inch/16-cm cake tin, taking care that there are no holes in the pastry and that it is not too thick at the corners.

Put half the salmon in the bottom of the pie and even it out. Spoon in the onion and mushroom mixture and cover with the remaining salmon. Mash the anchovy fillets. Melt the remaining butter, add the mashed anchovy and pour this over the salmon.

Take the remaining pastry and roll it out to the size of the top of the pie. Wet the edges and cover the pie. Make a hole in the middle and decorate with pastry trimmings. Brush with the beaten egg and cook for 45 minutes in a moderately hot oven (190°C/375°F/Gas Mark 5). Remove from the oven and allow the pie to cool in the tin for at least 15 minutes before turning out.

Serve warm or cold.

POACHED TURBOT WITH PINK SAUCE

Like cod, turbot came into its own in Victorian times. But whereas the cod's flesh was usually minced into a forcemeat and used to stuff its head, turbot was cooked whole in specially-shaped fish kettles. It was then served either hot or cold, garnished with a rich cream sauce flavoured with shrimps, oysters or lobster coral.

This recipe is equally good hot or cold and should be accompanied by rice or a plain green salad in order not to mask the delicate flavour of the turbot.

2 fillets of turbot (one fillet should be sufficient for 2 people)
4 oz/100 g onion, sliced
2 slices lemon
6 black peppercorns
5 fl oz/150 ml white wine
1 oz/25 g butter
2 oz/50 g button mushrooms, sliced
4 oz/100 g prawns or shrimps, shelled
2 oz/50 g cockles or clams, shelled
2 fl oz/50 ml brandy
4 egg yolks
7 fl oz/200 ml double cream
salt and white pepper

Serves 4

Put the fillets in a large pan with the onion, lemon slices, peppercorns and wine and just enough water to cover the fish. Bring to the boil and simmer for 10–15 minutes or until the fish is cooked. Transfer the fillets to a serving dish and reserve the stock.

Melt the butter in a pan and gently fry the mushrooms. Add the prawns or shrimps and cockles or clams. Stir well and add the brandy and 7 fl oz/200 ml of the fish stock. Beat the egg yolks into the cream and add both to the sauce. Heat gently, stirring continuously until the sauce thickens – do not boil or the sauce will curdle. Season to taste with salt and white pepper and spoon over the fish.

Serve hot or cold.

CARP WITH GAMMON

'Cookery is like matrimony,' Yuan Sin, the gastronomic sage of the East is said to have declared. 'Two things served together should match.' And surprisingly, the unlikely combination of ingredients in this very Dickensian recipe 'match' extremely well.

1 large carp, cleaned and filleted
4 thin gammon steaks, approximately 4 oz/100 g each
2 oz/50 g butter
4 oz/100 g onions, finely chopped
7-oz/210-g can of smoked oysters or clams
8 fl oz/225 ml red wine

Serves 4

Lay the fillets of carp and the gammon steaks on a baking rack, dot with 1 oz/25 g of the butter and cook under a hot grill for approximately 5 minutes or until both are cooked. If the gammon steaks are thicker than the carp they may need slightly longer. Remove to a heated serving dish and keep warm.

Meanwhile, in a saucepan melt the butter with the oil from the fish can and gently fry the onion until soft. Chop the oysters or clams and add them, with the wine, to the saucepan. Boil briskly for a couple of minutes and spoon over the carp and gammon. Serve at once.

DEVILLED WHITEBAIT

A 'whitebait dinner' was a delicacy indulged in by certain Victorian gentlemen who foregathered, in the season, at the Trafalgar tavern in Greenwich. Here, the dinner conformed to the strictest rules:
    'The dinner is to consist of turtle soup followed by no other fish but whitebait, to be succeeded by no other meat but grouse, which are to be succeeded simply by apple fritters and jelly, pastry on such occasions being completely out of place. With the turtle of course there will be punch, with the whitebait, champagne and with the grouse claret. I shall permit no other wines unless perchance a bottle of port . . .'

> 1 lb/450 g fresh or frozen whitebait
> ½ teaspoon cayenne pepper
> 1 oz/25 g seasoned flour
> oil for deep frying
> 1 lemon, quartered
> thinly sliced brown bread and butter

Serves 4

Wash the whitebait and dry thoroughly. Mix the cayenne with the flour and lightly coat the fish with the mixture.
    Heat the oil in a deep frying pan until it sizzles when you drop in a small piece of bread. Put a quarter of the fish in a basket, lower them into the oil and fry until they are crisp and brown but not burnt. Turn onto kitchen paper to drain, then keep warm in a serving dish. Repeat until all the fish are cooked. If you want the fish to be very fiery, sprinkle over another ½ teaspoon of cayenne.
    Serve at once with lemon wedges and plenty of brown bread and butter.

MACKEREL WITH GOOSEBERRY SAUCE

The frequent appearance of gooseberries, apples and currants in recipes for meat and fish is explained by the fact that all fruits, and acidic ones in particular, have certain antiseptic properties. This may have little relevance today but when there were no refrigerators to keep meat and fish fresh, a built-in 'antiseptic' did much to alleviate the consequences of eating old and possibly tainted food.

3 large mackerel, cleaned
4 slices fennel
4 slices lemon
small bunch of chopped chives or spring onions
8 black peppercorns
10 fl oz/300 ml dry white wine
8 oz/225 g fresh or frozen gooseberries (not canned)
1 oz/25 g butter
5 fl oz/150 ml double cream
juice of 1 small lemon
lemon slices, to decorate

Serves 6

Put the mackerel in an ovenproof dish with the fennel, lemon, chives and peppercorns. Add the wine, cover and bake in a moderate oven (180°C/350°F/Gas Mark 4) for 20–30 minutes, or until the fish is cooked. Remove the fish, cool it, skin it and fillet it. Strain the cooking liquid and reserve.

Stew the gooseberries very slowly in the butter until very soft. If you like the sauce smooth, sieve the fruit, otherwise liquidise it. Add the cream, lemon juice and 2 or 3 spoonfuls of the reserved liquor – the sauce should be the consistency of thick cream. Arrange the fillets in a dish and spoon the sauce over them. Decorate with lemon butterflies. Serve cold.

The dish can also be served hot but, if so, the fish and the sauce should be heated separately and the latter poured over immediately before serving.

ARNOLD BENNETT OMELETTE

This very Edwardian dish was invented by the Savoy hotel for the novelist and critic, Arnold Bennett, one of whose passions in life was smoked haddock.

8 eggs
4 tablespoons water
salt and pepper
12 oz/350 g cooked smoked haddock
4 oz/100 g well-flavoured cheese, grated
5 fl oz/150 ml double cream
½ oz/15 g butter
freshly ground black pepper

Serves 4

In a bowl, beat the eggs with the water and season well. Flake the smoked haddock and mix in the grated cheese and half the cream.

Heat the butter until sizzling in a large omelette pan. Pour in the egg mixture and start to cook as for an omelette. When the eggs are half-cooked, scrape them into a preheated ovenproof flan dish. Spread the cheese and haddock mixture over the egg, pour over the remaining cream and sprinkle with a little freshly ground black pepper.

Put the dish under a hot grill for approximately 4 minutes to heat the fish and cheese and finish cooking the eggs. Serve at once.

BERTIE WOOSTER'S KEDGEREE

'*There we really had breakfast . . . fried eggs, scrambled eggs, bacon, fishcakes and kedgeree, sometimes mushrooms, sometimes kidneys . . .*'

Today it seems hard to believe that the Victorians and Edwardians actually disposed of all that food at breakfast. But whether it was eaten or not, kedgeree, with its strange amalgam of north country smoked haddock and Indian rice and curry, was de rigueur on any gentleman's breakfast table.

    12 oz/350 g smoked haddock fillets
    6 tablespoons long grain rice
    1 small onion
    4 oz/100 g butter
    6 oz/175 g raisins
    ½ teaspoon curry powder (strong)
    1 hard-boiled egg
    juice of 1 lemon

Serves 6

Poach the fish for 10 minutes in gently boiling water; drain and flake. Cook the rice in boiling water for 11 minutes, until it is cooked but not too soft; drain and rinse in more boiling water. Chop the onion finely and fry it gently in 1 oz/25 g of the butter until soft but not coloured. Pour boiling water over the raisins and soak them for 10 minutes.

Take either a double boiler or an ovenproof dish with a lid. Put the fried onion in the bottom and cover with the raisins, and then with the fish. Melt the rest of the butter and mix it with the curry powder to make a paste. Mix this well into the rice and spoon it over the fish.

Cover the dish with a tea-cloth and then with the lid so that it is well sealed. If in a double boiler, simmer for 25 minutes; if in a casserole, cook in a slow òven (150°C/300°F/Gas Mark 2) for 25 minutes.

To serve, heat a flat dish and turn the kedgeree out onto it so that the fish, raisins etc are uppermost. Finely chop the hard-boiled egg, sprinkle it over the top and pour over the lemon juice. Serve at once.

Meats ~ spitted, sodden, baked & rolled

MEDIEVAL BLANCMANGER

A medieval blancmanger's only relationship to the wobbly, pink dessert that the name conjures up in the twentieth-century mind is the fact that both should be eaten with a spoon! In the Middle Ages, a 'blancmanger' meant what it said – a white thing to eat. Moreover, a luxurious 'white thing', for it was made from expensive imported almonds and rice, and chickens that should have been alive, earning their keep by laying eggs . . .

Forks did not come into regular use in England until the seventeenth century, and it was important that made-up dishes like this could be eaten with a spoon.

12 oz/350 g cooked chicken meat
3 oz/75 g pudding rice
1½ oz/40 g ground almonds
5 fl oz/150 ml milk
2 fl oz/50 ml single cream
½ oz/15 g castor sugar
salt
½ oz/15 g browned flaked almonds

Serves 6

Pull the cooked chicken apart and pound the meat to a paste in a food processor, or use a pestle and mortar if you are feeling energetic!

Cook the rice for 10 minutes in boiling water and drain.

Mix the almonds, milk and cream to a smooth paste and put in a shallow saucepan. Add the rice and chicken. Simmer gently, stirring continually, until the mixture thickens. Add sugar and salt to taste. Spoon into a dish or mould and chill until an hour before it is required.

Before serving, decorate with flaked almonds. The blancmanger should be served cold but not chilled.

'YSTEWED PYGEIONS'

Pigeon was among the most popular of medieval dishes. Unlike farmyard animals, so many of which had to be killed off in the autumn owing to a shortage of winter fodder, pigeons could forage for themselves even in the hardest weather. Indeed, by February or March they were often the only kind of fresh meat available.

These stewed pigeons, and the bread plate or 'trencher' which had soaked up the gravy, would have been eaten with the fingers.

6 pigeons
4 oz/100 g brown breadcrumbs
6 large cloves of garlic, finely chopped
1½ teaspoons thyme
1 teaspoon marjoram
2 teaspoons parsley, chopped
1 teaspoon savory
salt and pepper
2 eggs
½ teaspoon each ground ginger and ground cloves
juice of 1 lemon
10 fl oz/300 ml red wine
2 pints/1.2 litres strong brown stock
6 thick slices of wholemeal bread (these can be lightly fried in butter)

Serves 6

Clean out and dry the pigeons. Mix the breadcrumbs, garlic, herbs and seasoning in a bowl. Add the eggs to bind and mix well. Fill the birds with the stuffing.

Place the pigeons in a heavy-based saucepan just big enough to hold them. Mix the spices with the lemon juice, add the wine and stock and pour over the pigeons. Cover and bring to the boil. Simmer gently for 2 hours, by which time the pigeons should be very tender.

Put the bread on the serving dish and place one pigeon on each piece.

Season the sauce to taste and reduce a little if necessary by boiling it briskly for a few minutes. Pour the sauce over the pigeons just before serving.

CAPON OR TURKEY ROAST IN HONEY

Turkeys did not become really popular until the eighteenth century, but capon has been a 'feast-day' dish since the earliest times. In 1378 a roast capon cost only a penny less than a roast goose at a pie shop, while 'best capon baked in pastry' cost as much as a roast pig. The same obliging shop would also cook the capon if the customer had no such facilities: 'For the fire, paste and trouble upon a capon provided by the customer — 1½d.'

The honey glaze used in this recipe was a medieval favourite. Honey is unique in its ability to penetrate the skin of an animal, no matter how thick, thus rendering the flesh tender and sweet while glazing the skin as it cooks.

1 capon or small turkey
the liver from the bird, chopped
1 oz/25 g butter
1 medium-sized onion, finely chopped
large handful of parsley, finely chopped
3 oz/75 g cooking apple, peeled and chopped small
3 oz/75 g plump raisins
juice and rind of 1½ lemons
3 oz/75 g ground almonds
3 oz/75 g brown breadcrumbs
1 teaspoon each ground ginger and salt
½ teaspoon black pepper
1 egg
2 oz/50 g butter
2 tablespoons honey

Serves 8–10

Remove the giblets from the bird, retain the liver and discard the rest. Melt the butter in a saucepan, add the onion, liver and parsley and fry gently until the onion is soft and the liver firm. Take off the heat and add the apple, raisins, lemon, almonds, breadcrumbs, seasoning and the egg. Mix well.

Stuff the bird at both ends and secure with a skewer. Place in a roasting pan. Melt the honey and butter together and spoon over the bird; as it cools it will cling fairly well to the skin. Leave the bird to marinate in the honey in the refrigerator or larder (uncovered) for 24 hours, spooning over any excess mixture now and then.

Roast in a moderate oven (180°C/350°F/Gas Mark 4), basting frequently with the honey and butter mixture, for approximately 20 minutes to the pound (450 g). The skin will gradually turn black and shiny in contrast to the very white meat beneath.

Serve either warm or cold.

SPICED BRISKET

Spicing and pickling are among the oldest ways of preserving meat. The joint would be immersed in salt for several days, then soaked in a pickling solution based on strong preservatives such as saltpetre, vinegar, brown sugar and treacle. Spices, herbs and flavourings were added according to the type of meat and personal preference. Once the pickles had penetrated right through the joint, it would be taken out of the solution and, again depending on the meat and the locality, be either dried or smoked.

The strength of the pickling agents was gauged according to their preservative powers, not their flavour. The result was that many pickled meats tasted unpalatably strong, hence the prevalence of strong, sweet sauces to counteract the salt and the pickle. In this recipe the pickle has been adapted to modern taste.

4 lb/1.8 kg lean, boned brisket of beef
10 oz/275 g sea salt
2 spring onions
3 bay leaves
1 level teaspoon saltpetre
1 level teaspoon each allspice, cloves, nutmeg and mace
1 level teaspoon each chopped thyme and mint
$\frac{1}{2}$ teaspoon black pepper
4 tablespoons dark brown sugar

Wipe the boned brisket with a damp cloth and place in a china bowl – do not use metal of any kind. Rub the meat well on all sides with 8 oz/225 g of the salt, cover with a tea-cloth and leave in a cool place (a larder rather than a refrigerator) for 24 hours.

Peel the onions, and chop finely with the bay leaves. Mix with the rest of the ingredients. Each day rub this mixture into the meat (using rubber gloves if your hands are in any way sensitive), pouring off any liquid that may have formed in the bottom of the bowl. It should take 7 days to use up all the spicing mixture.

At the end of this time, place the brisket on a board and roll it lengthways, without wiping off any of the spices that have stuck to the meat. Tie it neatly. Put it in a heavy-based saucepan or iron casserole and cover it with warm water. (If you have a fish kettle, this is ideal for cooking the brisket.) Simmer it over a low heat for 2 hours and leave it to cool in the liquid. Remove the meat and set it between two plates with a heavy weight on top; press it for 8 hours.

When the brisket is pressed, remove the plates and chill it well before serving.

There should be approximately 3 lb/1.35 kg of meat, which should serve 12 people.

MEDIEVAL PORK STEW

This recipe is drawn from a collection of 'gentlemanly cookery copied of the serjeant to the king' – hence its use of expensive currants and almonds. Not all royal households indulged themselves in such luxuries; Henry II's, for example, was notorious for its meanness. The king was obsessed with the fear of getting fat, so ate very sparingly himself and paid little attention to his table. The result was that provisions were scanty, badly cooked and often tainted, while the wine was 'so full of dregs that courtiers were compelled to close their eyes and filter it through their teeth.'

> 2 oz/50 g beef dripping or butter
> 3 medium-sized leeks, cleaned and thickly sliced
> 3 turnips, peeled and diced
> 1 large onion, peeled and chopped
> 2 lb/900 g stewing pork, cubed
> 1 teaspoon each ground mace and salt
> ¼ teaspoon each ground cloves and black pepper
> bouquet garni
> 2 oz/50 g currants, washed
> 20 fl oz/600 ml red wine
> 20 fl oz/600 ml beef stock
> 2 oz/50 g whole almonds

Serves 6

Melt half the fat in a frying pan and lightly brown the vegetables. Transfer the vegetables to a deep saucepan with a slotted spoon. Trim the pork and fry it quickly in the remaining fat. Transfer the meat to the saucepan. Add the spices, seasoning, bouquet garni and currants, stir well, and then add the wine and stock.

Bring to the boil and simmer for 1 hour. Add the whole almonds and simmer for another 15 minutes.

Adjust the seasoning to taste and serve.

ELIZABETHAN BEEF BALLS

The danger with all 'hashed' or made-up dishes is that they are so easy to adulterate – and the more seasoning and flavouring they contain, the easier it is! Not that the 'local authorities' were unaware of the problems. Town and city councils were continually passing ordinances to prevent butchers selling meat by candlelight lest they should 'sell a piece of an old cow for a chop of a young ox, or wash old meat that hath hung weltering in the shop with new blood.'

1½ lb/700 g minced beef
½ teaspoon each ground cloves, black pepper and mace
1 teaspoon salt
5 oz/150 g brown breadcrumbs
1½ oz/40 g currants, washed
1 egg
approximately 2½ pints/1.5 litres beef stock

Serves 6

Mix together the beef, spices and seasoning, breadcrumbs and currants. Add the egg and beat well. Form the mixture into walnut-sized balls and set aside.

Heat the stock until simmering. Gently drop the balls into the stock with a slotted spoon and poach for 4–5 minutes. Drain on kitchen paper.

The balls should be reheated briefly in the oven and served with chutneys or relishes.

SIR HUGH PLAT'S POLONION SAWSEDGES

Sir Hugh Plat would have stuffed his 'sawsedge meat' into a 'great sheepes' gut' and hung it in the fireplace to smoke, thus preserving it for up to a year.

If you can persuade your butcher to give you some sausage skin and you have a wood fire, you can do the job properly — but even unsmoked they are, as Sir Hugh says, 'good with sallats, to garnish boyled meates or to make one relish a cup of wine.'

1 lb/450 g good sausage meat
1 small onion, very finely chopped
1½ teaspoons ground ginger
1 teaspoon freshly ground black pepper
1 teaspoon ground coriander
1 teaspoon ground nutmeg
1 teaspoon ground cloves
2 teaspoons savory, dried
2 teaspoons thyme, dried
1 teaspoon parsley, fresh if possible
1 teaspoon chervil, dried
flour
1 oz/25 g butter

Serves 4

Mix well the sausage meat with the onion and all the spices and herbs. Form the mixture into small cakes and roll in flour. Fry gently in the butter for approximately 4 minutes or until they are cooked.

STEWED BEEF WITH ANCHOVY DUMPLINGS

In the twentieth century, cattle are scientifically fed to ensure that their flesh will not be tough; in a less scientific age butchers and cooks relied on the method of killing the animal to 'tenderise' its meat. Pigs and calves were often flayed before they were slaughtered; salmon (for fish, too, were subjected to these cruel methods) were hacked up, live, into collops or cutlets. Bulls were thought to make better eating if they had been 'baited'; indeed, in the sixteenth century, butchers faced prosecution for selling 'unbaited bull'.

A modern and more humane way to ensure your beef is tender is to set it aside to mature in a refrigerator or larder for at least 24 hours after it has been cooked. This also deepens and improves the flavour.

1 oz/25 g butter
4 oz/100 g onions, chopped
4 oz/100 g bacon, diced
1½ lb/700 g stewing beef, trimmed and diced
16 anchovy fillets, chopped
15 fl oz/450 ml red wine
15 fl oz/450 ml beef stock
6 black peppercorns
4 oz/100 g brown breadcrumbs
handful of parsley, chopped
2 eggs

Serves 6

Melt the butter and briskly fry the onion, bacon and 8 anchovy fillets until coloured but not burnt. Remove to a deep pan with a slotted spoon and quickly fry the meat in the remaining fat to seal. Transfer the browned meat to the pan. Add the red wine, stock and peppercorns, bring to the boil and simmer for 1 hour or until the beef is tender.

Mix the remaining anchovy fillets with the breadcrumbs and parsley. Beat the eggs and stir into the crumb mix. Form chestnut-sized dumplings out of the mixture.

To serve, reheat the stew. When almost at boiling point, add the dumplings and simmer briskly for a further 10 minutes. Serve at once.

'TO MAKE A STEAKE PYE WITH A FRENCH PUDDYNGE IN IT'

A suet or forcemeat dumpling, known in the seventeenth century as a French pudding, was often served with meat to help eke it out. In this recipe, which dates from 1658, the ever-popular orange juice was used to moisten the pie rather than gravy.

6 small sirloin steaks
salt and freshly ground black pepper
nutmeg
6 oz/175 g sausage meat
3 oz/75 g breadcrumbs (preferably brown)
1 teaspoon each thyme and parsley, dried
½ teaspoon savory
2 oz/50 g suet, finely chopped
salt and pepper
2 oz/50 g raisins
1 egg, beaten
1 lb/450 g shortcrust pastry
1 oz/25 g butter
juice of 2 oranges
1 egg, to glaze

Serves 6

Sprinkle the steaks with salt, freshly ground black pepper and nutmeg and set aside.

In a bowl, mix the sausage meat, breadcrumbs, herbs and suet. Season with salt and pepper, add the raisins and then the beaten egg to bind. Form the mixture into 10–12 small round dumplings and set aside.

Roll out the pastry in one piece so that it will line a pie dish sufficiently large to hold the steaks and dumplings, and also fold over the top to make the lid (rather like a Cornish pasty).

Line the pie dish with the pastry, leaving the ends hanging over the side; put in the steaks and dumplings alternately, dot with the butter and squeeze over the juice of 2 oranges. Bring up the edges of the pastry and pinch them together as for a pasty, trim and brush with beaten egg. Cook in a moderate oven (180°C/350°F/Gas Mark 4) for 1 hour or until the pastry is well browned.

THOMAS DAWSON'S STEWED STEAKS

'The befe of Englande,' says Sir Thomas Elyot in A Castel of Helthe, *published in 1538, 'bringeth stronge nourishmente to those that are in helthe.' He would undoubtedly have approved of this dark, rich dish which appears in Thomas Dawson's* Good Housewife's Jewel *of 1585. The addition of dried fruits is very reminiscent of the Middle Ages, as is his direction to 'serve the steakes on soppes', or thick slices of bread, designed to soak up the gravy. In the Middle Ages these hunks of bread, or 'trenchers' as they were called, were often used as plates and could be eaten after the meat. If not eaten, they were thrown in the 'alms bowl' to be distributed to the poor after the meal!*

4 × 8-oz/225-g sirloin steaks
14 fl oz/400 ml beer or ale
14 fl oz/400 ml red wine
bouquet garni
2 small onions, finely chopped
4 cloves
small piece of ginger root
½ stick cinnamon
6 black peppercorns
1 oz/25 g dark brown sugar
1 oz/25 g raisins
8 prunes, halved and stoned
4 slices wholemeal bread, fresh or toasted

Serves 4

Put the steaks in a wide saucepan, add the wine and beer and bring quickly to the boil – skim off any skum that rises. Add the bouquet garni, onion, cloves, ginger root, cinnamon and peppercorns. Cover and simmer gently for 15 minutes. Remove the steaks with a slotted spoon, place each one on top of a piece of bread and keep warm.

Add the sugar, raisins and prunes to the juices in the pan and boil fast for 3 minutes. Pour the fruits and juices over the steaks and serve immediately.

SIR HUGH PLAT'S VEAL IN A SHARP SAUCE

In the Middle Ages, veal was not a popular dish, for it was thought grossly extravagant to kill a calf, unless it was diseased, when that calf could grow up to be a much larger working cow or bull. However, by the end of the seventeenth century, animal husbandry had improved so much that veal was in quite common use. Samuel Pepys included a loin of veal in a dinner party menu in 1659 and Parson Woodforde, in the eighteenth century, often indulged in a fillet of veal or veal cutlets.

Sir Hugh Plat's recipe, which dates from 1609, in fact suggests veal or chicken and there is no reason why you should not substitute the latter.

1 oz/25 g butter
1 lb/450 g well-trimmed pie veal or 4 chicken joints
½ lettuce, finely chopped
large handful of parsley, chopped
4 oz/100 g spinach, well washed and chopped
2 oz/50 g leeks, chopped
5 fl oz/150 ml dry white wine
10 fl oz/300 ml light veal or chicken stock
2 fl oz/50 ml wine vinegar
¼ teaspoon mace
black pepper

Serves 4

Heat the butter in a deep frying pan. Fry the meat briskly until lightly browned, then add the vegetables, spices and liquids. Cover the pan and simmer gently for 25 minutes.
 Adjust seasoning and serve at once.

VENISON STEWED IN BEER

For many centuries venison formed the centrepiece of almost any noble feast, not so much because of its flavour as a meat but because the noble host's main enjoyment in life was hunting it! Henry VIII enclosed over 1700 acres of village land around his palace of Nonesuch and stocked them with deer; James I swapped his manor at Hatfield for his Lord Chancellor's manor at Theobalds because he thought the hunting was better. Even George III thought nothing of spending the day in the saddle in pursuit of his quarry. If a lady was a member of the hunt it was her privilege to make the first cut in the dead animal, which was then handed over to the huntsman to cut up and bring home.

2 lb/900 g stewing venison
15 fl oz/450 ml real ale or beer
2 oz/50 g butter
1½ lb/700 g parsnips, peeled and diced
½ oz/15 g seasoned flour
1 tablespoon black treacle
1 oz/25 g dark brown sugar
1 tablespoon red currant jelly
salt and pepper

Serves 4

Trim the venison and marinate for 1 hour in 7 fl oz/200 ml of the beer.

Melt 1 oz/25 g of the butter in a pan and lightly brown the parsnips; transfer to an ovenproof casserole. Drain the venison and reserve the marinade. Toss the meat in the seasoned flour and fry briskly in the remaining butter to seal. Transfer to the casserole.

Add any remaining flour to the juices in the pan, cook for a minute and then gradually stir in the marinade, and add the black treacle, sugar and the remains of the beer. Pour over the meat in the casserole.

Cover and cook in a slow oven (150°C/300°F/Gas Mark 2) for 1½–2 hours, depending on the venison.

Remove from the oven, add the red currant jelly, stir well and adjust the seasoning before serving.

MRS BLENCOWE'S FORCED LEG OF MUTTON

In Mrs Blencowe's recipe one is instructed to 'take a large leg of Mutton and cut all ye meat out leaving ye skin whole; then take ye meat and shred it very small with halfe a pounde of suet.' If this seems rather a drastic way to treat a leg of mutton, one should remember that in 1694 the sheep that provided it would have spent several years developing its leg muscles up hill and down dale, and might well have needed to be 'shred very small' to render it edible!

1 large leg of lamb
½ oz/15 g butter
2 oz/50 g onion, finely chopped
2 oz/50 g suet, chopped
1 teaspoon dried thyme
4 fresh sage leaves, chopped
10 fresh mint leaves, chopped
10 rosemary leaves, chopped
1 sprig fresh rosemary
2 oz/50 g ground almonds
1 oz/25 g fresh or frozen red currants or, if not available, fresh or frozen cranberries
salt and pepper
1 egg

Sauce:
1 oz/25 g butter
½ oz/15 g cornflour
5 fl oz/150 ml red wine vinegar
10 fl oz/300 ml chicken or veal stock
small handful of parsley, chopped

Serves 6

Cut the bone out of the leg of lamb, taking quite a lot of the meat with it. Remove this meat from the bone. Cut more flesh from the inside of the leg until there is about 2 in/5cm of flesh left attached to the skin all round. Chop all the extra meat finely.

Melt the butter in a pan and gently cook the onion until soft but not coloured. In a bowl mix the onion, chopped lamb, suet, herbs, almonds and fruit and season well with salt and pepper. Beat the egg and thoroughly mix it into the forcemeat, or stuffing.

With a skewer secure the hoof end of the leg to the main part of the joint. Push all the forcemeat into the hole, close the edges as well as possible and tie with string. Four or five loops will be necessary to hold the forcemeat in place.

Put the lamb in a baking tray (sitting on the sprig of rosemary) and bake in a moderate oven (180°C/ 350°C/Gas Mark 4) for 20 minutes to the pound (450 g), total weight.

To make the sauce, melt 1 oz/25 g butter in a pan. Add the cornflour and cook for a couple of minutes. Gradually add the stock and vinegar mixed, and the parsley. Bring to the boil and simmer for 3 minutes.

To serve, cut the string from the lamb and serve hot, in slices. The sauce should be served separately as an accompaniment. It is very piquant and only a small amount will be needed to flavour the lamb.

PATRICK LAMB'S PUPTON OF PIGEONS

Patrick Lamb was master cook at Queen Anne's court and many was the feast prepared under his watchful eye. Queen Anne herself had a great weakness for good food (although chocolates and sweetmeats were her especial favourites) and her court banquets were the envy of her royal contemporaries. Indeed, Patrick Lamb maintained that 'our credit and esteem with foreign ministers has been in great measure built and supported on this foundation.'

A pupton was a rich and meaty terrine, cooked very slowly and nearly always served cold.

4 pigeons
2 oz/50 g butter
15 fl oz/450 ml brown stock
15 fl oz/450 ml red wine
2 sweetbreads, cleaned and quartered
4 pickling onions, peeled
2 oz/50 g mushrooms
10 whole, cooked chestnuts
salt, pepper and nutmeg
$\frac{1}{2}$ oz/15 g flour
1 large onion, finely chopped
1 lb/450 g sausage meat
small handful of parsley, chopped
1 teaspoon thyme, dried
juice of $\frac{1}{2}$ lemon
salt and pepper
7–10 rashers of bacon
juice of 1 orange
large bunch of watercress

Serves 10

Clean the pigeons and fry in $1\frac{1}{2}$ oz/40 g of butter to brown. Transfer the pigeons to a saucepan and add the stock and wine. Cover and simmer for 45 minutes or until the pigeons are almost cooked.

Meanwhile, fry the sweetbreads and pickling onions in the remaining butter. Add them to the pigeons, with the mushrooms, 6 chestnuts and the seasoning, and simmer for a further 15 minutes.

Remove the pigeons from the pan and bone them, keeping the flesh in as large pieces as possible. Remove the vegetables, sweetbreads, chestnuts and mix with the pigeon meat.

In a small bowl, add a little of the stock to the flour to make a paste and add gradually to the stock. Boil briskly to thicken and reduce.

In the remaining butter, fry the chopped onion and add to the sausage meat with the herbs and remaining chestnuts, roughly chopped. Add the lemon juice and season with salt and pepper.

Line a 6-inch/15-cm loose-bottomed cake tin, or a soufflé dish, with the bacon rashers. With two-thirds of the forcemeat, pack the bottom and sides of the tin. Pile the pigeon mixture in the middle, flatten it and pour in 5 fl oz/150 ml of the thickened stock. Cover the pupton with the remaining forcemeat and smooth over the top with a knife.

Cover and bake for 45 minutes in a moderate oven (180°C/350°F/Gas Mark 4). Cool.

When quite cold, loosen the edges and turn the pupton out onto a serving dish. Just before serving, squeeze over the juice of the orange and surround with watercress.

ROAST TURKEY WITH ORANGE & ARTICHOKE HEART SAUCE

The term 'turkey' was applied to many things of obviously foreign origin in the fifteenth and sixteenth centuries, since the vast majority of exotic foreign goods came via that country. And so it was with the overgrown chicken, which came to be known as a 'turkey cock'. Although they are seldom to be found on menus prior to 1650, by the early eighteenth century Daniel Defoe was describing great 'droves of turkeys' being marched seventy to eighty miles from villages in Norfolk to Leadenhall market.

As with so many eighteenth-century meat recipes, the bird is roasted and the sauce served as an accompaniment.

1 oz/25 g butter
8 oz/225 g onions, very finely sliced
3 stalks celery, chopped small
8 oz/225 g fresh cooked, canned or frozen artichoke hearts,
    quartered
15 fl oz/450 ml chicken or turkey stock
4 oranges
salt and pepper
1½ lb/700 g roast turkey, sliced

Serves 6

In a pan melt the butter and add the onions and celery. Cook very slowly until the onions are quite soft but not coloured. Add the artichoke hearts, turkey stock, rind and juice of 2 oranges. Bring to the boil and simmer for 5 minutes. Season to taste with salt and pepper.

Lay the turkey out on a serving dish, cover and heat through in a warm oven. Segment the remaining oranges and add to the sauce.

Just before serving, reheat the sauce and spoon it over the turkey.

WILLIAM VERRAL'S HIND
QUARTER OF LAMB

Marinades of various kinds appeared frequently in eighteenth-century recipes because they helped to break down the tougher fibres of the meat without disguising its flavour.

1 small leg of lamb
2 cloves of garlic, peeled and slivered
2 pints/1.2 litres milk
2 teaspoons coriander seeds
1 teaspoon salt
10 black peppercorns
handful of parsley, chopped
6 spring onions, chopped
juice of 1 lemon
1 lb/450 g spinach

Serves 6

Cut several gashes in the lamb and insert the garlic. Mix the milk, coriander, salt, peppercorns, parsley, onion and lemon juice in a bowl large enough to hold the lamb. Marinate the lamb in the mixture for 1 hour.

Remove the lamb from the marinade and roast it in a moderate oven (180°C/350°F/Gas Mark 4) for 1¼ hours.

Put the marinade in a large saucepan with the spinach, which has been thoroughly washed and trimmed. Bring to the boil and cook briskly for 5 minutes.

Chop the spinach roughly, with the marinade. Return to the saucepan and boil briskly for approximately 30 minutes or until the sauce is substantially reduced – there should be plenty of it but the spinach should not be afloat!

Line a serving dish with the spinach and sauce. Immediately before serving, carve the lamb, arrange the slices on the bed of spinach and 'send' it to the table.

'BALONS OF THE LEGS OF FOWLS'

Boning and stuffing things has always been a favourite occupation of the aspiring cook. In the Middle Ages no feast table was complete without a galantine: a large bird such as a swan, boned, and stuffed with a smaller bird such as a capon, which, in turn, had been stuffed with a smaller bird, and so on down to a lark.

William Verral gives recipes for boning legs of lamb and pork as well as legs of chickens, although he does not suggest (as he does for the chickens) that one should leave the feet on!

If you wish to follow his instructions exactly 'take out the thigh and leg bone to the knee without cutting the skin; let the feet continue on and scald or burn off the stocking but take care not to burn the skin.' Then continue with the recipe as given below. To serve, you must 'dish them up with the feet to them' – preferably all sticking up around the serving dish with a pool of sauce in the middle!

        6 whole chicken legs
        1 oz/25 g butter
        salt and pepper
Stuffing:
        1 oz/25 g butter
        1½ oz/40 g bacon, diced
        1½ oz/40 g onions, finely chopped
        1 oz/25 g fennel, finely chopped
        handful of parsley, chopped
        1 oz/25 g ground almonds
        2½ oz/65 g brown breadcrumbs
        1½ oz/40 g cooked cockles
        ½ teaspoon ground ginger
        rind and juice of 1 orange
        1 egg yolk
        salt and pepper
Sauce:
        1 oz/25 g flour
        10 fl oz/300 ml good chicken stock
        5 fl oz/150 ml dry white wine
        juice of 2 oranges
        salt and pepper

Serves 6

Carefully remove the bones from the chicken legs without breaking the skin, if possible.

Melt 1 oz/25 g butter in a pan and gently cook the bacon, onion and fennel until soft. Put them in a bowl and add the parsley, almonds, breadcrumbs, cockles and ginger. Mix well, then add the orange juice and rind beaten with the egg yolk. Season to taste.

Push as much stuffing as possible into each leg and secure well with wooden cocktail sticks or skewers.

Put the legs into a baking tin, dot with 1 oz/25 g butter, sprinkle with salt and pepper and roast in a moderate oven (180°C/350°F/Gas Mark 4) for 45 minutes.

Place the balons on a serving dish, carefully removing the skewers or sticks.

Add the flour to the pan juices and cook for a couple of minutes. Gradually add the stock and wine, scraping all the bits off the bottom of the pan. Add the orange juice and season to taste. Strain.

Serve the balons hot accompanied by the sauce.

PETTY PATTIES OF VEAL SWEETBREADS

Offal was popular in the Middle Ages and in later periods. It was stuffed with herbs and oatmeal into sheep's stomachs to make haggis-like puddings, or mixed with blood to make black puddings.

As the quality and availability of meat improved, offal fell from favour. Sweetbreads, however, retained their popularity and Parson Woodforde, who noted in his diary 'a very elegant dinner' where 'rosted sweetbreads' were served between a 'Fillet of Veal with Mushrooms and hot Lobster' would undoubtedly have appreciated William Verral's recipe.

12 oz/350 g shortcrust pastry
1 lb/450 g sweetbreads, soaked and cleaned
juice of ½ lemon
½ oz/15 g bacon fat
3½ oz/90 g mushrooms, sliced
3½ oz/90 g ham, finely chopped
12 spring onions, chopped
12 gherkins, sliced thinly
2 teaspoons parsley, chopped
pinch of salt, black pepper and nutmeg
2 fl oz/50 ml single cream
juice of 1 orange and 1 lemon
1 egg, beaten

Serves 6

Line six small flan cases with two-thirds of the pastry.

Simmer the sweetbreads with the lemon juice in just enough water to cover them for 5 minutes; drain and chop roughly. Melt the bacon fat and lightly fry the mushrooms. Add these to the sweetbreads along with the ham, spring onions, gherkins, parsley and seasoning. Pile this mixture into the flan cases.

Mix together the cream, orange and lemon juice and divide it between the flans.

Roll out the remaining pastry and cover the 'patties'. Decorate each with the pastry trimmings, and brush with beaten egg. Cook for 25 minutes in a moderately hot oven (190°C/375°F/Gas Mark 5).

HANNAH GLASSE'S DUCK WITH CUCUMBER

Hannah Glasse was cooking and writing some eighty years after Charles II and his courtiers had returned from their long exile at the court of Louis XIV, where they had developed a taste for French 'haute cuisine'. By her day, the controversy over the comparative virtues of French and English cooking had reached its height. As a good Englishwoman she had no time for French cookery with its 'costly and pernicious sauces and absurd mixtures'. And even more did she deplore the 'blind folly of an age which would rather be imposed on by a French booby than give employment to a good English cook!'

True to her creed, her recipes are simple but draw out the natural flavours of her ingredients.

2 large onions, peeled and very finely chopped
3 cucumbers, peeled and diced
10 fl oz/300 ml claret
2 duckling
1 oz/25 g butter
1 oz/25 g flour
10 fl oz/300 ml chicken or duck stock
salt and pepper (sea salt and freshly ground black pepper if possible)

Serves 6

Put the onion and cucumber in a bowl and marinate in the claret for 2 hours.

Meanwhile, prick the duck all over and roast (on a rack) in a moderate oven (180°C/350°F/Gas Mark 4) for approximately 20 minutes to the pound (450 g).

Drain the vegetables, reserving the marinade. Melt the butter in a pan and briskly fry the onion and cucumber for a couple of minutes without colouring. Add the flour and cook for a further 2 minutes. Add the reserved marinade and the stock, bring to the boil and simmer for 10 minutes. Season to taste with salt and black pepper.

Carve the ducks and serve the sauce separately.

'TO BAKE A HARE'

This recipe comes from the diary of Ann Hughes, a farmer's wife in the last years of the eighteenth century. Her spelling and phraseology are so irresistible that it seems a shame not to quote her instructions in full:

'Tomorrow be our harvest home, so todaye Sarah, me and carters wiffe have been bussie with cooking divers goodies. . . . I did cook 3 hares, my dear mothers waye. After taking off their skinnes and pulling out their insides, I did cut them up in peeces, and lay in milk for one hower; while I did chop up 4 apples, 2 unions, a handful of lemmon tyme, sum lemmon rinde, pepper and salt, 3 hard boiled eggs, 3 sage leaves and a tee spoon of browne sugger. This be all chopped up together. Then I do put a laire of peeces of hare in a deep dish, then cuvver with the mess. Then a tabel spoon of water, and more hare, and a sprinkel more of the mixed mess till the dish be full. When 3 partes full, I do pore in 2 wine glass off porte wine. I do then take 4 eggs and beat up verrie well with 2 tablespoone of fresh cream, and a little salte; which I do pore in the dish after the hare hav been cookeing 2 hower and a half; keeping it covvered, ande putting back until the eggs be well set. This be verrie nice cold.'

1 hare, skinned and jointed
2 pints/1.2 litres milk
2 medium-sized onions, peeled and roughly chopped
4 medium-sized eating apples, peeled, sliced and diced
3 hard-boiled eggs, roughly chopped
rind of 2 lemons
2 teaspoons lemon thyme
½ teaspoon sage
1 teaspoon dark brown sugar
salt and pepper
10 fl oz/300 ml port
2 eggs
watercress

Serves 12

Put the hare in a bowl with the milk and leave to marinate for 1 hour. Transfer both to a large saucepan, bring slowly to the boil, skim and simmer for 1 hour. Cool the hare in the milk. Lift from the pan, take the meat from the bones and chop roughly; reserve the cooking milk.

Mix together the onion, apple, hard-boiled eggs, lemon rind, herbs, sugar and seasoning.

Put half the hare in the bottom of a casserole or pie dish. Cover with half the apple and onion mixture, and then with the rest of the hare. Pour in the port. Cover the hare with the remaining apple and onion mixture and smooth the surface. Mix 2 eggs with 2 tablespoons of the cooking milk, season well and pour over the top.

Cover and bake for $1\frac{1}{2}$ hours in a moderate oven (180°C/ 350°F/Gas Mark 4). Remove from the oven and let the pupton, or terrine, cool completely. When cold, turn it out onto a serving dish and surround with watercress.

PORC EN BALON

The original version of this recipe suggests that you take a whole pig and 'cut him open from head to tail'. In the eighteenth century, no-one ever bought less than half an animal.

1 boned blade of pork
Stuffing:
    4 oz/100 g sausage meat
    2 oz/50 g ham, cut in matchsticks
    1 stalk celery, finely chopped
    yolks of 3 hard-boiled eggs, mashed
    3 gherkins, chopped
    1 teaspoon dried sage
    juice and rind of 1 lemon
    salt and pepper
Sauce:
    3 oz/75 g onion, finely chopped
    1 teaspoon dried sage
    ½ oz/15 g butter
    2 teaspoons whole-grain mustard
    handful of parsley, chopped
    juice and rind of 2 oranges
    10 fl oz/300 ml chicken stock
    salt and pepper

A 4 lb/1.8 kg joint will serve 8 people

In a bowl mix the sausage meat, ham, celery, egg yolks, gherkins, 1 teaspoon dried sage, and the lemon rind and juice until they are well blended. Season with salt and pepper and stuff the pork with this mixture. Secure with a skewer and tie the joint firmly.

Roast in a moderately hot oven (190°C/375°F/Gas Mark 5) for 30 minutes to the pound (450 g). If you want crisp crackling, make sure the skin is dry and rub it lightly with oil and sprinkle with salt.

For the sauce, cook the onion and 1 teaspoon of sage gently in the butter until the onion is soft.

Add the mustard, parsley, orange rind and juice and stock. Bring to the boil and simmer for a couple of minutes. Season to taste and serve with the pork.

'FRIGGASIE OF CHICKENS'

Dishes combining meat and fish did not appear until the eighteenth century. For at least a century after the Reformation of the 1530s well over one hundred days in the year were non meat-eating fast days when only fish or eggs were allowed, with the result that fish was kept for fish days and meat for meat days.

4 oz/100 g butter
1 lb/450 g leeks, trimmed and finely sliced
½ cucumber, diced
1 small lettuce, washed and chopped
2 oz/50 g anchovies, chopped
1 chicken, jointed
2 oz/50 g flour
5 fl oz/150 ml dry white wine
10 fl oz/300 ml chicken stock
1 teaspoon thyme
freshly ground black pepper
4 oz/100 g mussels, frozen and thawed, or fresh and cooked
5 fl oz/150 ml single cream
juice of 1 lemon
2 egg yolks

Serves 4

Melt 2 oz/50 g of the butter in a heavy frying pan. Add the leeks, cucumber, lettuce and anchovies and cook gently until the vegetables are beginning to soften. Transfer the vegetables to an ovenproof casserole.

Melt the remaining butter in the frying pan, toss the chicken joints in flour and fry them briskly until they are well browned. Place them in the casserole on top of the vegetables. Add the white wine and stock, the thyme and the black pepper.

Cook for 30 minutes in a moderate oven (180°C/350°F/ Gas Mark 4).

Heat the mussels in the cream and add the lemon juice; take off the heat. Beat the egg yolks and add them to the mussel mixture. Pour this sauce over the chicken in the casserole and serve at once.

STUFFED ROAST TRIPE

'"It's a stew of tripe", said the landlord, smacking his lips, "and cow-heel," smacking them again, "and bacon," smacking them once more, "and steak", smacking them for the fourth time, "and peas, cauliflowers, new potatoes, and sparrow-grass, all working up together in one delicious gravy." Having come to the climax, he smacked his lips a great many times, and taking a long hearty sniff of the fragrance that was hovering about, put on the cover again with the air of one whose toils on earth were over.'

William Gelleroy's recipe does not totally conform to the landlord's ideal in Dickens's The Old Curiosity Shop, *but the result is not far off.*

    1 lb/450 g tripe, in one piece if possible
    2 oz/50 g butter
Stuffing:
    3 small onions, peeled and chopped
    3 rashers bacon, diced
    3 oz/75 g button mushrooms, sliced
    3 oz/75 g ham, diced small
    2 oz/50 g butter
    grated rind of 1½ lemons
    pinch each thyme and rosemary
    1½ teaspoons each chopped parsley and chopped chives
    5 oz/150 g brown breadcrumbs
    juice of 2 small oranges
    2 eggs, beaten
    salt, pepper and nutmeg
Sauce:
    2 large onions
    8 cloves
    1 pint/600 ml milk
    1 oz/25 g butter
    1 oz/25 g flour
    salt and pepper

Serves 6

Stuffing: Fry the chopped onion, bacon, mushrooms and ham in the butter for several minutes or until the onion and bacon are cooked and just beginning to turn colour.

Add the lemon rind, herbs, breadcrumbs and orange juice and mix well. Add the beaten egg and season with salt, pepper and nutmeg.

Lay the tripe flat on a board, lay the stuffing down the middle, roll up and tie with string. Rub the butter over the outside of the rolled tripe and roast in a moderately hot oven (190°C/375°F/Gas Mark 5) for 35 minutes.

Meanwhile, chop the onion and add it with the cloves to the milk. Bring to the boil, then take off the heat and allow to infuse for 30 minutes. Remove the cloves. Melt the butter in a pan, add the flour and cook for 2 minutes, then slowly add the milk with the onions and bring to the boil, stirring continuously. Cook for a couple of minutes until the sauce thickens.

Take the tripe from the oven, and cut the roll into fairly thick slices; place them in a serving dish and keep warm. Add the dripping from the roasting pan to the sauce and cook for another minute or two. Season to taste. Spoon the sauce over the tripe just before serving.

CHINO CHILO

Although the English taste for curried dishes dates mainly from the days of the British raj, firey, spiced stews were enjoyed in Tudor and Stuart times. In fact, there were two 'receipts' for curry powders in the rolls of Richard II's master cooks as early as 1390. None the less, most of the recipes, such as this one, were devised by the cooks and wives of civil servants in India in the heyday of the British Empire — inspired, no doubt, by the writings of Colonel Kenny Herbert, the greatest nineteenth-century authority on Indian curries.

8 oz/225 g patna or long grain rice
2 oz/50 g butter
1 tablespoon curry powder
1 large onion, finely chopped
1 lb/450 g lamb fillet, trimmed and cut into small cubes
1 bunch spring onions, chopped
10 fl oz/300 ml chicken stock
5 oz/150 g petit pois, fresh or frozen
½ cabbage lettuce, shredded
salt and pepper

Serves 4

Cook the rice, drain and keep warm.

Meanwhile, melt the butter in a saucepan and add the curry powder, stir together for a couple of minutes over the heat. Add the onion and lamb and fry briskly for about 3 minutes without burning. Add the chopped spring onion and stock, cover and simmer for 30 minutes.

If the peas are fresh, add them and cook for a further 5 minutes. Then add the lettuce, stir well and serve immediately, surrounded by a border of rice.

If the peas are frozen, add the peas and lettuce together and cook for 2 minutes before serving.

Serve with pickles and chutneys.

HAM & APPLE PIE

Until the twentieth century, the size and fatness of a pig, or of any other animal, went far to guaranteeing its desirability! William Cobbett regarded a pig that could walk 200 yards as 'not well fatted', while Parson Woodforde reported a sight-seeing expedition, with his friend Mr Ferman, to see a pig which 'was said to weigh 50 stones, to be 9 foot from the tip of his tail to the top of his snout and 4 foot high when standing.' Hams would often weigh over 20 pounds, leaving a tremendous amount of meat to be 'used up' after the first few meals, hence the usefulness of a slightly unusual and tasty dish like this ham and apple pie.

1 oz/25 g butter
8 oz/225 g onions, roughly chopped
8 oz/225 g parsnips, peeled and sliced
1 lb/450 g cooked ham, diced
8 oz/225 g cooking apples, peeled and sliced
salt and pepper
½ oz/15 g dark brown sugar
5 fl oz/150 ml cider
8 oz/225 g wholemeal shortcrust pastry
1 egg

Serves 4

Melt the butter in a saucepan and fry the onion and parsnip until they are lightly coloured but not burnt. Put a layer of this mixture in the bottom of an 8-inch/20-cm pie dish. Cover with half the ham and then with the apple. Sprinkle with salt and pepper and the sugar. Cover the apple with the rest of the ham and then with the rest of the onion mixture.

Top the pie with the pastry, decorate with the pastry trimmings and brush with beaten egg.

Cook in a moderately hot oven (190°C/375°F/Gas Mark 5) for 25 minutes or until the pastry is cooked and lightly browned.

ELIZA ACTON'S SAUSAGE CAKES WITH CHESTNUTS

The combination of sausage meat and chestnut is unusual but makes, as Miss Acton says in her recipe, an excellent dish, even in the adapted form in which it appears here. Eliza Acton's Modern Cookery *was published in 1845 and formed the basis for almost all Victorian cookery books, although, alas, the debt was seldom acknowledged. In the 1855 edition of the book she comments bitterly on the 'unscrupulous manner in which large parts of my volume have been appropriated by contemporary authors' – Mrs Beeton was among the worst offenders.*

1 lb/450 g sausage meat made up into 8 cakes
flour
1 oz/25 g butter
1 small can (5 oz/150 g) whole chestnuts
1 onion, peeled and chopped very fine
½ teaspoon cayenne pepper
7 fl oz/200 ml beer
salt and pepper

Serves 4

Roll the sausage cakes in flour and fry gently in butter for 10 minutes or until they are cooked through. Put them in a serving dish and keep warm, reserving the fat in which they have been fried.

Add the onion to the fat and cook gently until soft. Add the chestnuts (drained), the cayenne and the beer. Simmer gently for 5 minutes. Season to taste with salt and pepper and spoon over the sausage cakes.

Serve at once.

'A SHAPE OF VEAL'

In Scotland, most cooks had no time for those English epicures who, as Dr Kitchiner said, 'cannot endure the sight of the best bill of fare unless it is written in pretty good bad French.'

Mr Williamson's recipe is simple and well-flavoured. It is taken from Williamson's Cookery, *published in Edinburgh in 1877.'*

1 lb/450 g pie veal, trimmed
8 oz/225 g cooked ham, diced
4 oz/100 g onions, roughly sliced
4 oz/100 g carrots, sliced
6 black peppercorns
small handful of parsley, chopped
10 fl oz/300 ml dry white wine
20 fl oz/600 ml water
1 hard-boiled egg, sliced
6 slices of beetroot
8 gherkins, sliced
½ oz/15 g gelatine
beetroot or watercress to decorate

Serves 6

Put the veal, ham, vegetables, peppercorns and parsley in a saucepan with the wine and water. Bring to the boil, skim and simmer for 30 minutes.

Arrange the hard-boiled egg, beetroot and some gherkin slices in a pattern on the bottom of a pie or soufflé dish.

Remove the veal and ham from the heat, strain, reserving the stock. Discard the vegetables. Arrange the meat in layers in the pie dish with the rest of the gherkins.

Strain the stock through muslin until it is quite clear. Soften the gelatine in 2 fl oz/50 ml of the stock, then add a further 18 fl oz/500 ml of stock and heat until the gelatine has melted. Cool until almost cold but not set and pour slowly into the dish.

Cover and chill until set firm. When set, loosen the edges with a knife and turn out onto a serving dish. To decorate, surround with beetroot or watercress.

ELIZA ACTON'S BEEF CAKE

'Using up' was the Victorian cook's nightmare. In a large household, it could take the whole week to dispose of a twenty-pound Sunday joint. Often she must have repeated the old rhyme: 'Hot on Sunday; cold on Monday; hashed on Tuesday; minced on Wednesday; curried on Thursday; broth on Friday; cottage pie on Saturday.'

Miss Acton's cake would probably have appeared somewhere in the middle of the week!

approximately 10 rashers of bacon
1 lb/450 g minced beef
6 oz/175 g beef suet, finely chopped
4 oz/100 g onions, finely chopped
2 oz/50 g mushrooms, chopped
1 oz/25 g brown breadcrumbs
½ teaspoon each salt, ground mace and cloves
¼ teaspoon cayenne pepper
3 fl oz/75 ml beef stock

Serves 8

Line an 8-inch/20-cm loaf tin with the bacon rashers. Mix together the beef, suet, onion, mushrooms and breadcrumbs and season with the spices. Spoon into the loaf tin and smooth the top. Pour in the beef stock.

Cover the tin and bake in a bain marie in a moderate oven (180°C/350°F/Gas Mark 4) for 2 hours.

Cool. When completely cold, loosen the edges with a knife, turn the cake out and serve with salads.

BOILED MUTTON & CAPER SAUCE

'Although roasting and boiling are the most common and generally considered the easiest and most simple processes of cookery, it requires more unremitting attention to detail to perform them perfectly well than it does to make most made dishes.' So says Dr Kitchiner in his Cook's Oracle, published in 1804, and how right he is. Nothing will rescue an over-cooked joint of meat, whereas a dollop of cream or brandy will work miracles with a failing casserole or sauce!

1 leg of mutton (if available) or mature lamb – approximately
    12 oz/350 g uncooked weight per head
1 large onion, chopped
1 carrot, sliced
1 stick celery, sliced
6 black peppercorns
bouquet garni
2 oz/50 g butter
2 oz/50 g flour
3 fl oz/75 ml double cream
4 tablespoons capers, chopped
3 sprigs parsley, chopped
salt and pepper

Put the lamb or mutton in a pot just large enough to hold it. Add the onion, carrot, celery, peppercorns and bouquet garni and just enough water to cover the meat. Bring to the boil, skim, cover and simmer for 20 minutes to the pound (450 g).

When cooked, transfer the meat to a serving dish and keep warm; reserve the stock.

Melt the butter in a pan, add the flour and cook for a couple of minutes. Gradually add 20 fl oz/600 ml of the stock in which the meat was cooked. Bring to the boil and simmer until the sauce thickens. Add the cream, capers and parsley, cook for 2 minutes and adjust the seasoning to taste.

Coat the joint with approximately one-third of the sauce and serve the rest separately.

This amount of sauce should be sufficient for 6 portions.

Roots, Salats, Herbs & Vegetables

RICHARD II'S SALAT OF HERBS & CRESSES

In the time of Richard II no distinction was drawn between herbs and vegetables, both being known by the generic title of potherbs. Of the hundreds of herbs in regular cultivation, cresses were among the most popular. To quote Culpeper on the subject of watercress: 'Watercress is a good remedy to cleanse the blood in the spring and consume the grosser humoures that winter has left behind. Those that would live in health may use it if they please; if they will not I cannot help it!'

1 small green cabbage, finely sliced
1 bulb fennel, finely sliced
1 small leek, finely sliced
2 tablespoons fresh parsley, chopped
1 tablespoon fresh borage, chopped (if available)
$\frac{1}{2}$ tablespoon each fresh mint and sage leaves, chopped
1 teaspoon each fresh rosemary leaves and rue, chopped
sea salt and freshly ground black pepper
3 tablespoons cider vinegar
1 large bunch watercress
1 carton mustard and cress

Serves 6

Mix all the vegetables and herbs, except the cresses, in a salad bowl. Sprinkle with the salt, pepper and vinegar, toss and leave for 1 hour in a cool place.

Just before serving, break up the cresses and completely cover the other vegetables with a green carpet of cress.

STEAMED HERB PUDDING

Puddings that could be steamed over a cauldron already bubbling with a soup or stew were popular for the obvious reason that they cost nothing to cook. In poorer households, particularly in the cities where fuel was hard to come by, this was a great advantage. The ingredients were cheap, or to be had for the picking in the hedgerows, and the result would satisfy the most ravenous of hungers.

2 oz/50 g brown breadcrumbs
2 oz/50 g fine oatmeal
1 oz/25 g suet, chopped
2 oz/50 g leek or onion, chopped
2 teaspoons each of dried, or 4 teaspoons each of fresh, parsley
    and thyme, chopped
1 teaspoon each of dried, or 2 teaspoons each of fresh, sage, basil
    and savory, chopped
1 teaspoon black pepper
2 teaspoons sea salt
7 fl oz/200 ml water

Serves 4

Mix well all the dry ingredients and bind together with the water. Turn the mixture into a bowl, cover tightly and steam for 1 hour.

Turn out onto a warmed dish and serve at once.

'FRITTERS OF SPINNEDGE'

This recipe for spinach fritters appears in Thomas Dawson's Good Housewife's Jewel *of 1585 and, as in most Tudor recipes, no quantities are given. Since there were no weighing scales in the sixteenth century it was not possible to give accurate weights, so the inventor of a recipe had to rely far more heavily on the judgement and experience of the individual cook than he would today.*

2 lb/900 g spinach, washed and trimmed
5 oz/150 g brown breadcrumbs
1 egg
$\frac{1}{2}$ teaspoon each ginger and cinnamon
$\frac{1}{4}$ teaspoon each nutmeg and black pepper
1 teaspoon dark brown sugar
$1\frac{1}{2}$ oz/40 g currants, washed
$1\frac{1}{2}$ teaspoons salt
1 egg
6 oz/175 g flour
10 fl oz/300 ml real ale or beer
cooking oil or lard

Serves 6

Cook the spinach briskly in a little boiling water for 3 minutes; drain and chop roughly with a knife or in a food processor. Put the spinach in a bowl with the breadcrumbs, egg, spices, sugar and currants and beat together thoroughly. Season to taste with salt. Roll the spinach into small balls and set aside.

To make the batter, put the egg in a bowl and gradually mix in the flour and the beer, beating continually (either by hand or in a food mixer) to prevent lumps forming. Set aside for 30 minutes.

To cook, heat the oil or lard in a deep frying pan. Drop the fritters in the batter, coat well with the mixture, remove with a slotted spoon and drop into the oil. Fry briskly for approximately 2 minutes (depending on the size of the balls), remove with a slotted spoon and drain on some kitchen paper.

Serve immediately.

PARSNIP PUFFS

'Parsneps,' wrote Sir Kenelm Digby, Master of the Wardrobe to Charles I's wife, Henrietta Maria, 'cut into little pieces, is the best food for tame rabets, and makes them sweet' – but whether in temperament or in taste we are not told.

    1 lb/450 g parsnips
    2 oz/50 g brown breadcrumbs
    juice of 1 orange
    1 tablespoon medium sherry
    1 teaspoon dark brown sugar
    1 egg yolk
    salt, pepper and freshly grated nutmeg
    2 egg whites
    2 oz/50 g butter

Serves 6

Peel the parsnips, boil or steam them until they are soft and purée them in a blender or food mill. Add the breadcrumbs, orange juice, sherry, sugar, egg yolk and seasoning and beat well.

Whisk the egg whites until stiff but not dry and fold into the parsnip purée. Form the mixture into small cakes about 2 in/5 cm in diameter.

Heat the butter in a large frying pan and gently fry the puffs in the butter until browned but not burnt on both sides. Serve at once.

JOSEPH COOPER'S FRIED ARTICHOKES

'Artichokes,' says Dr Moufet, one of Queen Elizabeth's physicians, in his book on Health's Improvement, *'with oyl and vinegar, salt and pepper, gratefully recommend a glass of wine at the end of Meals. 'Tis not very long since this noble thistle was so rare in England that it was commonly sold for crowns apiece.'*

Joseph Cooper lived about sixty years after Dr Moufet, but the artichoke had obviously not lost its popularity.

> 2 cans (28 oz/800 g) artichoke hearts or 12 fresh artichoke hearts, cooked
> 2 oz/50 g seasoned flour
> 1 oz/25 g butter
> 2 oranges

Serves 4

Drain and dry the artichoke hearts and toss in the seasoned flour. Melt the butter in a frying pan and fry the hearts gently until they are heated through and slightly browned all over. Transfer them to a serving dish and keep them warm.

Segment 1 orange and mix with the artichoke hearts. Squeeze the other orange and add the juice to the butter in the pan. Reheat and pour over the hearts immediately before serving.

MUSHROOM & ORANGE SALAD

Oranges were known in England all through the Middle Ages but it was only in the seventeenth century that they were successfully cultivated in the magnificent orangeries of the great country houses. Samuel Pepys first saw them growing on Lord Brooks's estate in Hackney in the year of the Great Fire, 1666, and he was so fascinated by them that he 'pulled one off by stealth (being mighty curious of them) and ate it . . .'

    8 oz/225 g mushrooms
    salt and pepper
    3 oranges
    ½ lettuce
    4 tablespoons French dressing
    2 oz/50 g walnuts, chopped

Serves 4

Wash or wipe the mushrooms and quarter them. Sprinkle them with salt and pepper and squeeze over the juice of 1 orange. Peel the remaining 2 oranges, remove all pith and segment them.

Wash the lettuce and make a bed of it in a shallow serving dish.

Mix the orange segments with the mushrooms and toss them in the French dressing. Pile the mixture onto the lettuce and sprinkle the chopped walnuts over the top.

RADISHES AU BLOND

As with many of our root vegetables, radishes were well-known by the sixteenth and seventeenth centuries; James I's apothecary, John Parkinson, gives instructions for their cultivation along with carrots, turnips, parsnips, artichokes and even potatoes, the latest exotic import from the New World.

In Tudor and Stuart times the radishes would normally have been served raw in a salad or 'salat'; this rather unusual recipe for cooked radishes comes from the eighteenth century.

6 bunches of radishes
6 large or 12 small spring onions, chopped
12 black peppercorns
15 fl oz/450 ml chicken stock
½ teaspoon salt

Serves 6

Trim and wash the radishes, and halve the larger ones so that they are all approximately the same size. Put them, with the onion, peppercorns and stock in a saucepan. Bring to the boil and simmer, uncovered, for 20–30 minutes until they are cooked but still crisp. Season to taste with salt and serve in their juice.

CANDIED POTATOES

'The universally adored and ever popular potato,' complained Captain Gronow in his memoirs, published in 1861, 'produced at the earliest period of the dinner, was eaten with everything right up to the sweets.'

Since the English ability to ruin good vegetables by bad cooking was well-known, the Captain probably had some justification for his complaint. He had obviously never tried this eighteenth-century recipe for candied potatoes.

2 lb/900 g potatoes, peeled and thinly sliced
3 oz/75 g butter
salt and pepper
4 fl oz/100 ml Madeira or sweet sherry
1 oz/25 g dark brown sugar

Serves 4

Brown the sliced potatoes in the butter and then place in layers in an ovenproof casserole, sprinkling each layer with salt and pepper. Pour over the wine, cover and bake in a moderate oven (180°C/350°F/Gas Mark 4) for 45 minutes. Remove the lid and sprinkle the sugar over the potatoes. Return to the oven and cook for a further 15 minutes, uncovered.

STEWED CUCUMBERS

'When the season of the year is,' says Culpeper in his Herbal of 1653, 'take the cucumber and bruise him well and distill the water from him. The face being washed with the same water cures the reddest face that is. It is also excellently good for sunburning, freckles and morphew . . .'

If you would rather eat the cucumber than apply it to your face, Dr Kitchiner's recipe is fresh and unusual. And, as he says, 'if rubbed through a tamis or fine sieve, this would be entitled to be called "cucumber sauce".'

3 cucumbers, peeled and dried in a cloth
4 tablespoons flour
12 small white onions, peeled
1 oz/25 g butter
2 tablespoons oil
10 fl oz/300 ml light chicken or veal stock
salt and pepper

Serves 6

Heat the butter with the oil in a saucepan until the butter is melted.

Quarter the cucumbers lengthwise, de-seed them and then cut them into 2-inch/5-cm lengths. Dust the cucumber pieces lightly in the flour and brown them, with the onions, in the butter and oil. Add the stock, cover the saucepan and simmer gently for 15 minutes.

Remove the vegetables to a heated serving dish using a slotted spoon, and reduce the sauce by boiling briskly for 5–10 minutes. Adjust the seasoning and pour over the cucumbers before serving.

SHERRIED POTATOES

It has been said that the reason potatoes were cultivated so much earlier in Ireland than in England (where they did not become popular until the nineteenth century) was that they mature below the ground, whereas cereal crops mature above. This means that they are far less easily destroyed by marauding armies than are wheat or barley. When a country was invaded and overrun as often as Ireland was between the sixteenth and the twentieth centuries, this could clearly have been an advantage.

3 lb/1.35 kg potatoes
3 oz/75 g butter
1 oz/25 g granulated sugar
½ teaspoon each nutmeg, black pepper and salt
2 eggs
4 fl oz/100 ml medium sherry
juice and grated rind of 2 small oranges
1 oz/25 g nibbed almonds

Serves 6

Peel and boil the potatoes. When they are cooked, drain them and mash them with butter, sugar and seasoning.

Beat the eggs and mix them with the sherry, orange juice and orange rind, and then beat them into the potatoes. Finally mix in two-thirds of the almonds and pile the mixture into a soufflé dish. Sprinkle the remaining almonds on top and bake for 20 minutes in a moderately hot oven (190°C/375°F/Gas Mark 5) until the potato is lightly browned on top.

ARTICHOKE MOULD

Whether it was a hangover from earlier centuries when raw vege-
tables were considered dangerously indigestible, or whether it was
purely their own preference for smooth, puréed textures, the Vic-
torians seldom garnished their 'cold tables' with raw vegetable
salads. They chose to cook and mash their ingredients, forming them
into shapes and moulds which could then be glazed and decorated.

So it was with this artichoke mould – an excellent accompaniment
to a strong-flavoured meat such as ham.

1 lb/450 g Jerusalem artichokes, cleaned and trimmed
7 fl oz/200 ml milk
1 oz/25 g butter
1 oz/25 g flour
1 teaspoon granulated sugar
salt and pepper
2 egg yolks
3 fl oz/75 ml thick, well-flavoured mayonnaise
a few sliced mushrooms or watercress leaves to decorate

Serves 4

Put the artichokes in a saucepan with the milk, bring to
the boil and simmer until quite soft. Remove from the
heat, drain and purée the artichokes with 3 fl oz/75 ml of
the milk.

Melt the butter in a saucepan, add the flour and cook
for a couple of minutes. Add the artichoke purée and sugar
and season to taste with salt and pepper.

Remove from the heat, add the egg yolks, mix well
together and pour into a well-greased mould or soufflé
dish, approximately 6 in/15 cm in diameter. Bake uncovered in a moderate oven (160°C/325°F/Gas Mark 3)
for 40 minutes or until the mould is quite set.

Remove from the oven and cool. When it is cold, loosen
the edges of the mould and turn out onto a serving dish.
Mask with the mayonnaise and decorate with sliced
mushrooms or watercress leaves.

ELIZA ACTON'S CARROTS IN THEIR OWN JUICE

'By the following mode of dressing carrots,' says Miss Acton, 'whether they be young or old, their full flavour and all the nutriment they contain are entirely preserved: and they are at the same time rendered so palatable with it that they furnish at once an admirable dish to eat without meat as well as with it. A simple but excellent receipt.'

2 lb/900 g carrots
1 oz/25 g butter
1 oz/25 g flour
handful of parsley, chopped
3 fl oz/75 ml single cream
salt and freshly ground black pepper
juice of 1 orange

Serves 6

Peel, trim and slice the carrots thinly. Put them in enough boiling, salted water to cover and cook until tender.

Meanwhile, soften the butter in a large bowl and mix with the flour, parsley and cream.

Drain the carrots, reserving 8 fl oz/225 ml of their cooking water. Add this liquid to the butter and cream mixture, stirring well to maintain a smooth texture. Add the carrots and return to the saucepan. Cook for a couple of minutes to thicken the sauce. Add the orange juice, black pepper and salt to taste and serve at once.

ELIZA ACTON'S FORCED 'TOMATAS'

'Tomatas' were almost unknown in England until the late nineteenth century, when they became a regular import from the United States of America. Even then, they were normally used as a fruit for jam rather than as a vegetable. Mrs Beeton, among others, treated them with great suspicion: 'The whole plant has a disagreeable odour and its juice, when subject to the action of fire, emits a vapour so powerful as to cause vertigo and vomiting.'

Happily, Miss Acton does not appear to have suffered from the same symptoms.

12 medium-sized tomatoes
12 anchovy fillets, chopped
2 medium-sized onions, finely chopped
1 oz/25 g butter
3 oz/75 g breadcrumbs
1 teaspoon thyme (dried)
black pepper

Serves 6

Cut the tops off the tomatoes and remove all the pulp.

Fry the anchovy fillets and onion in ½ oz/15 g of the butter until the onion is soft but not coloured. Add the breadcrumbs, thyme, black pepper and the tomato lids, chopped very small. Mix well and pile into the tomato shells. Dot the remaining butter over the tomatoes and put them under a medium grill for 7 minutes to cook the shells lightly and to brown the tops.

Serve warm or cold.

DRESSED BEETROOT

When the great Carême was working for the Prince Regent in the early 1800s, he found that 'in London there are many things which save the cook work; for example the vegetables arrive ready washed and prepared, although one pays dearly for them.'

In the case of beetroot, preparation would have meant boiling, so this little recipe would have saved time for the hard-pressed cook.

1½ lb/700 g cooked baby beetroots
3 oz/75 g butter
1 large onion, finely chopped
2 cloves of garlic, crushed
4 tablespoons parsley, finely chopped
6 tablespoons red wine vinegar
salt and pepper

Serves 6

Peel the beetroots, leaving them whole. Melt the butter and gently cook the onion and garlic until soft. Add the parsley, beets, vinegar, salt and pepper and simmer for 5 minutes, stirring occasionally.

The beetroot can be served either hot or cold.

VICTORIAN PEASE PUDDING

'A full belly to the labourer,' said William Cobbett, 'is the foundation of public morals and the only real source of public peace.'

Of all the foods that the labourer may have eaten, either by an open fire in his peasant's cottage or from a street stall in Victorian London, a dish of hot pease pudding (with or without the pork) must have done most to 'fill his belly'.

1 lb/450 g dried split peas
4 oz/100 g bacon, diced
1 medium-sized onion, finely chopped
2 pints/1.2 litres ham or chicken stock
2 oz/50 g butter
2 egg yolks
salt and pepper

Serves 6

Put the peas, bacon and onion in a saucepan with the stock. Bring to the boil and simmer for 1 hour or until the peas are 'mushy' and all the liquid absorbed. Beat in the butter and egg yolks and season to taste with salt and pepper. Turn into a basin and steam for 1 hour. Turn out and serve at once with more butter or gravy.

The traditional meat accompaniment to pease pudding is roast or boiled pork.

MRS MARSHALL'S CABBAGE & CAPER SALAD

Cabbage, the most common of our indigenous vegetables, has always formed a staple, and yet often despised, food of the English working man – 'loosening, if moderately boyled,' according to John Gerard, Lord Burghley's gardener in the time of Elizabeth I. Beau Brummell thought cabbage so coarse a food that he cut one aspiring young lady dead because he had actually seen her eat some!

    1 small, young green cabbage
    1 large onion, finely chopped
    small bunch of fresh tarragon, chopped
    3 tablespoons French dressing
    1 tablespoon double cream
    2 tablespoons capers
    1 hard-boiled egg, sliced

Serves 6

Wash the cabbage well, shred it and mix it with the onion and tarragon. In a bowl, mix the cream with the French dressing and in this toss the cabbage mixture. Turn into a salad bowl, sprinkle the capers over the top and decorate with sliced hard-boiled egg.

Desserts, Puddings, Entremets & Creams

FIFTEENTH-CENTURY CURD CHEESE TARTS

When no refrigerators were available in which to keep milk fresh, the only way to preserve it was to turn it into cheese; for long term storage into hard cheeses such as Cheddar, for short term, into cream and curd cheeses. The latter could be used as a dessert sweetened with honey, or, for the rich, with sugar grated from cones imported at enormous expense from the Middle East. Curd cheese also formed a splendid basis for the decorations so beloved of medieval cooks.

2½ pints/1.5 litres fresh unhomogenised milk
2½ teaspoons rennet
1 oz/25 g butter
2 oz/50 g digestive biscuits, crushed
1 oz/25 g castor sugar
½ oz/15 g ground almonds
pinch nutmeg
2 eggs
½ teaspoon orange flower water
1 teaspoon brandy
2 oz/50 g currants, washed
9-inch/23-cm pastry case, baked blind
dates or prunes, jams and jellies, for decoration

Serves 8–10

Warm the milk to blood heat and add the rennet. When the milk has congealed, stir it gently with a spoon, but try not to break up all the curds. Turn it into a jelly bag or a drainer made of muslin and leave overnight for the whey to drain off.

Rub the butter, crushed biscuits and sugar together. Add the almonds, nutmeg, orange flower water, brandy and eggs and beat thoroughly. Add the drained curds and mix well, then add the currants.

Pour the mixture into the pastry case and 'send it to the oven' (150°C/300°F/Gas Mark 2) for 20 minutes or until set and lightly browned.

When the tart is cold, draw out on its surface a pattern for the decoration. Make your dividing lines with thinly-sliced dates or prunes and fill the spaces with brightly coloured jams and jellies.

APPLEMOY

In classical times, all round fruits were called apples, but by the Middle Ages an apple did mean an apple. It is one of the few fruits indigenous to Great Britain.

Applemoy is an apple purée-cream, thickened with ground almonds and sweetened with honey.

1 lb/450 g cooking apples, peeled, cored and sliced
1 oz/25 g rice flour
1 oz/25 g ground almonds
½ teaspoon allspice
½ teaspoon ground cloves
1 tablespoon honey
10 fl oz/300 ml milk
ground cinnamon
5 fl oz/150 ml double cream

Serves 6

Simmer the apples in a little water until soft, and then purée them.

Put the rice flour, ground almonds, spices and honey in a saucepan. Gradually add the milk and bring to the boil. Simmer for 5 minutes, stirring all the time to prevent any lumps from forming; the mixture should be fairly stiff. Stir in the apple purée.

Serve either warm or cold with the cinnamon 'strewn' over the dish, and plenty of cream.

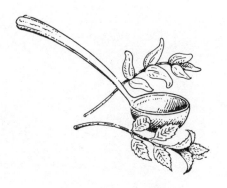

FRUMENTY

Porridge, the most traditional of all Scottish dishes, is a direct descendant of medieval frumenty. The main difference between the two is that Scotland is oats-and-barley country whereas most of England is wheat-growing.

In the Middle Ages the wheat, soaked in water or milk, depending on the season and the state of the cow, would be put in the communal village oven after the weekly bake. The residual heat would cause the wheat to 'cree' or swell and burst. If times were hard, it would then be eaten as it was; if the bees and the cow had been behaving well, honey and cream would be added.

    4 oz/100 g wheat germ
    15 fl oz/450 ml milk
    4 oz/100 g plump raisins
    2 oz/50 g dark brown sugar
    1 teaspoon each ground cloves and cinnamon
    8 fl oz/225 ml single cream

Serves 6

Put the wheat germ and milk in a bowl, cover and leave in a warm place for 24 hours for the germ to swell.

Put the swollen wheat germ in a saucepan and add the raisins, sugar, spices and cream. Bring to the boil and simmer for 5 minutes to thicken the mixture slightly.

Serve hot with cream and honey or more brown sugar.

POKEROUNCE

Pokerounce might well have been one of the dishes served at Henry VI's coronation in 1429, although in appearance it might have had difficulty in vying for attention with a 'custarde royale made with a leoparde of golde sityng thereone' or a 'fritour' or pancake 'made to look like the sun'. As regards taste, however, especially if made with fresh walnuts, it would have been hard to beat.

  5 fl oz/150 ml double cream
  ½ oz/15 g castor sugar
  3 tablespoons honey
  1 scant teaspoon each ground ginger and cinnamon
  ½ teaspoon cloves, ground
  3 oz/75 g broken walnuts
  4 slices hot, wholemeal toast

Serves 4

Lightly whisk the cream with the sugar.

Melt the honey with the spices, add the walnuts and boil for 2 minutes. Spoon over the toast and serve at once accompanied by the whipped cream.

BAKEWELL TART

The modern Bakewell tart is a direct descendant of the almond cheesecakes of the Middle Ages. This twentieth-century version is probably the richer, using butter and ground almonds in place of the medieval almond milk (achieved by lengthy boiling of sweet almonds in water) and cream or curd cheese.

8 oz/225 g shortcrust pastry
raspberry jam
4 oz/100 g butter
4 oz/100 g ground almonds
4 oz/100 g castor sugar
½ teaspoon almond essence
1 egg
milk

Serves 4

Roll out the pastry and line an 8-inch/20-cm flan case. Spread the bottom of the flan case with a ½-inch/1-cm layer of jam.

Melt the butter and add the almonds, sugar and almond essence. Remove from the heat, add the egg and beat well. Spoon the mixture over the jam in the flan case and smooth out. Use the pastry scraps to make a lattice work on top of the flan and brush with a little milk.

Bake in a moderate oven (180°C/350°F/Gas Mark 4) for 25–30 minutes or until the top is lightly coloured.

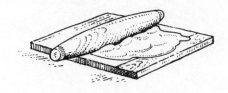

BRANDIED APPLE FRITTERS

As late as the seventeenth century it was thought dangerous to eat raw fruit, no doubt because seasonal fruit would be consumed in far greater quantities than unaccustomed stomachs could cope with. 'Raw fruits,' says Sir Thomas Elyot in his Castel of Helthe, *'are generally noyfulle to man and doe engender ylle humoures.' Once cooked, however, they were found to lose many of their laxative properties and were, accordingly, much used!*

4 cooking apples or tart eating apples, peeled, cored and thinly sliced
peel of 1 lemon
1½ oz/40 g castor sugar
½ teaspoon ground cinnamon
4 fl oz/100 ml brandy
3 oz/75 g butter
7 fl oz/200 ml double cream
dark brown sugar

Serves 4

Put the apples in a bowl with the lemon rind, sugar, cinnamon and brandy and leave to marinate for a couple of hours.

Melt the butter in a shallow frying pan and add the drained apple slices, reserving the juice. Fry briskly, but do not burn, until the apples are golden brown all over. Remove to a warm serving dish.

Remove the lemon peel from the brandy juice and add this liquid to the butter in the pan. Add the cream and heat through without boiling.

Serve the apples sprinkled with dark brown sugar and accompanied by a jug of the hot cream sauce.

CHARLES II'S CIDER SYLLABUB

Syllabubs came into their own during the reign of Charles II, who was addicted to them.

The name derived from an Elizabethan term for bubbling drinks, and originally that is exactly what a syllabub was – a clear wine with a froth of cream on top. However, a means of whisking cream was not discovered until late in the seventeenth century; until then the only way to create the froth was to 'drive' the cream or milk through the air, so it would gather bubbles as it went. What better way to achieve this than to milk the cow directly into the syllabub pot.

If a cow is to hand, by all means experiment; if not, a birch whisk achieves much the same effect!

juice and rind of 1 lemon
6 fl oz/175 ml cider
1 dessertspoon castor sugar
½ teaspoon grated nutmeg
3 fl oz/75 ml double cream
3 fl oz/75 ml single cream

Serves 4

Put the lemon rind in the cider and infuse overnight. Remove the rind and put the cider in a tall jug or container, add the sugar and nutmeg and stir well. Mix the creams and lemon juice and trickle them into the cider.

Take a birch whisk (if not available, an ordinary whisk or even an electric beater will give almost the same result) and whisk the mixture in the jug by rubbing the whisk backwards and forwards between your hands – you will find that the mixture froths much more than you expect. When it is thick and spongy, pour it into four glasses and leave for several hours before serving.

The cider should sink to the bottom so that you can drink it after spooning the froth from the top.

QUAKIN PUDDING

Mrs Blencowe's quakin' pudding must have been a great favourite in the farmhouse kitchen, where cream and eggs were to be had in abundance. Festivities among the yeomen and farmers of Tudor and Stuart times were always communal affairs, and lavish ones at that if one is to believe William Harrison:

'In feasting the husbandmen doo exceed after their manner; especially at bridals, purification of women and such odd meetings where it is incredible to tell what meat is consumed and spent, each one brings a dish or so many with him as his wife and he do consult upon, but always with this consideration, that the leefer (better) freend shall have the better provision.'

pinch of mace
10 fl oz/300 ml double cream
1 egg plus 1 egg white
1 oz/25 g flour
6 oz/175 g brown breadcrumbs
3 oz/75 g sugar
pinch of nutmeg
1 oz/25 g plump raisins
grated rind of 1 lemon
1 oz/25 g butter
5 fl oz/150 ml white wine

Serves 4

Add the mace to the cream in a saucepan, bring to the boil, turn off the heat and leave to infuse for 30 minutes.

In a bowl mix the flour, breadcrumbs, 2 oz/50 g of the sugar, nutmeg, raisins and lemon rind. Beat the egg and egg white, stir in the cream, then gradually add the liquid mixture to the dry ingredients and mix well. Turn into a basin, cover and steam for 1 hour.

For the sauce, melt the butter in a pan, add the remaining sugar and the wine, stir and cook for a couple of minutes to melt the sugar. Turn out the pudding onto a heated plate, pour over half the wine sauce and serve the rest of the sauce separately.

JOHN FARLEY'S TEA CREAM

When it first arrived in England in the late seventeenth century, tea was exotic, expensive and credited with medicinal virtues ranging from the cure of gout to the removal of fevers. So it was hardly surprising that tea leaves cropped up everywhere. One group of country ladies actually boiled the leaves and served them on toast with butter.

John Farley's recipe sounds scarcely less bizarre yet the flavour is unusual and pleasing — provided that you like China tea!

$\frac{1}{4}$ oz/10 g China tea leaves
15 fl oz/450 ml double cream
1 oz/25 g castor sugar
3 eggs

Serves 4

Put the tea leaves in a small saucepan with the cream, bring to the boil and allow to infuse for 10 minutes, then strain. Discard the tea leaves. Add the sugar and taste; if it is not sweet enough add a little more sugar.

Beat the eggs together, add to the sweetened cream and beat well. Pour into four ramekin dishes and cook for 25 minutes, or until the creams are set, in a cool oven (150°C/300°F/Gas Mark 2).

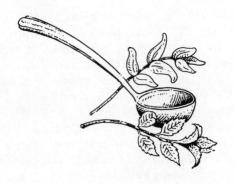

BOMBARD APPLES

In 1296 costard apples fetched one shilling per hundred and were regularly sold and exchanged at markets throughout the autumn months. Indeed, one man is recorded as having paid his rent in 'permain' apples as early as 1200.

In Tudor times 'pippins' were very popular spiced and baked, and not long after Mrs Blencowe had written her recipe (1694), Catherine the Great, Empress of all the Russias, was having golden pippins sent from England, each one wrapped in silver paper.

6 medium-sized, tart cooking apples
approximately 1½ lb/700 g shortcrust pastry
6–8 oz/175–225 g mincemeat
1 egg white
2½ oz/65 g icing sugar
½ teaspoon lemon juice

Serves 6

Core the apples but do not peel them. Divide the pastry into six pieces and roll out each piece thinly until it is large enough to envelop an apple.

Place an apple in the middle of each piece of pastry and fill its centre with mincemeat. Carefully fold up the pastry to enclose the apple, trimming the excess pastry and sticking the edges firmly together with a little water. Try not to break the pastry.

Place the apples on a tray and bake in a moderately hot oven (190°C/375°F/Gas Mark 5) for 30 minutes. Remove the apples and cool slightly.

Put the egg white, icing sugar and lemon juice in an electric mixer and whisk until the meringue is very shiny and stiff enough to hold its shape. Divide the meringue mixture into six and pile it on each apple, smoothing the top slightly and encouraging it to dribble down the sides.

Return the apples to a cool oven (130°/250°F/Gas Mark ½) and cook for a further 25 minutes to set the meringue. Serve warm.

'HOW TO MAKE A RISE PUDING'

It is only since the days of nannies, nurseries and boarding schools that rice pudding has become such a dreaded dish. A few hundred years ago quite the opposite was the case, for a 'rise puding' demanded all kinds of expensive and exotic ingredients: imported rice, oranges and lemons, cream and sack or sweetened wine.

In the original recipe it is suggested that the 'puding' be baked 'in a dish between two Puff Pastes', but I feel this might be a little too much for twentieth-century appetites!

    2 oz/50 g pudding rice
    10 fl oz/300 ml milk
    1 pinch each of ground cinnamon, mace and nutmeg
    1 oz/25 g candied peel
    1 oz/25 g plain sweet biscuits, grated
    $\frac{3}{4}$ oz/20 g dark brown sugar
    2 tablespoons orange juice
    1 fl oz/25 ml sweet sherry
    4 fl oz/100 ml single cream
    4 fl oz/100 ml double cream

Serves 4

Put the rice in a saucepan with the milk, bring to the boil and simmer for 10 minutes. Add the spices and peel, biscuits, sugar, orange juice, single cream and sherry. Stir well and turn into a pie or soufflé dish.

Bake uncovered in a moderate oven (180°C/350°F/Gas Mark 4) for 45 minutes. Serve hot with the double cream lightly whipped.

SIPPET PUDDING

Sippets were fingers of bread used for dipping or dunking in soups or gravies, so this eighteenth-century bread and butter pudding would, no doubt, have been made from left-overs from the previous evening's dinner. As white bread in the eighteenth century retained the germ in the wheat, the texture would have resembled our wholemeal bread.

1 oz/25 g butter
8 oz/225 g brown or good quality white bread, in slices, retaining
    the crusts
6 oz/175 g sultanas
3 oz/75 g suet, finely chopped
½ teaspoon ground nutmeg
3 oz/75 g dark brown sugar
2 eggs plus 3 yolks
12 fl oz/350 ml single cream
6 fl oz/175 ml sweet white wine
approximately 1 tablespoon castor sugar

Serves 6

Rub an 8-inch/20-cm pie dish with the butter. Line the bottom of the dish with half the bread and sprinkle over half the sultanas, suet and nutmeg and 1 oz/25 g of dark brown sugar. Cover with the rest of the bread and the remaining sultanas, suet, nutmeg and another ounce (25 g) of sugar.

Whisk the 2 whole eggs with 6 fl oz/150 ml of cream, add the remaining dark brown sugar and pour over the pudding. Cook in a moderate oven (160°C/325°F/Gas Mark 3) for 25 minutes or until the custard has set.

To make the sauce, whisk the 3 egg yolks in a bowl with the wine and the rest of the cream. Then continue whisking the mixture over boiling water until it thickens slightly. Add sugar to taste (the quantity will depend on the sweetness of the wine) and serve with the pudding. Both pudding and sauce should be warm but not too hot.

WILLIAM VERRAL'S CHERRY PROFITEROLES

Cherries were among the most venerable of English fruits. John Gerard mentions them as fillings for tarts and pies in Tudor times; Celia Fiennes comments on the cherries growing by the Thames in Kent at the end of the seventeenth century; and a hundred years later Horace Walpole waxes positively lyrical on the subject:

'My verdure begins to recover its bloom . . . I did not despair, for in this country, nobody pays his debts like rain. It may destroy flowers but one cannot complain of want of fruit; cherries, apples, walnuts are more exuberant than their leaves; I don't believe that a single blossom will fail coming of age. Cherries, I am told, are cried in London at half penny a pound – Kentish ones, I mean – which is cheaper than they have been since William the Conqueror landed there!'

1 oz/25 g butter
10 fl oz/300 ml water
grated rind of 1 lemon and juice of ½ lemon
1 oz/25 g castor sugar
pinch of salt
4 oz/100 g flour
2 eggs
1 lb/450 g black cherry jam
2 fl oz/50 ml cassis, cherry herring or cherry brandy
1 small tart apple, peeled, cored and very finely chopped
5 fl oz/150 ml double cream

Serves 6

Put the butter and water in a pan with the lemon rind and bring to the boil. Mix ½ oz/15 g of the sugar and a pinch of salt with the flour and tip into the boiling mixture. Beat thoroughly until well amalgamated. Add the eggs and beat again until shiny.

With a teaspoon, put walnut-sized spoonfuls of the mixture on a greased tray and bake in a moderately hot oven (190°C/375°F/Gas Mark 5) for 25 minutes or until the profiteroles are risen and lightly browned. Remove from the oven, and cool slightly.

Cut off the tops of the profiteroles with a sharp knife and remove any uncooked dough from the middle with a small teaspoon. When cold, fill the profiteroles with half the jam and replace the tops. Put them in an ovenproof serving dish, sprinkle with the remaining sugar and set aside.

In a small saucepan slowly heat the remaining jam until it has melted. Add the lemon juice, liqueur and the apple and cook for a couple of minutes without boiling.

To serve, heat the profiteroles gently. Reheat the sauce to just below boiling point and pour over. Serve immediately with lightly whipped cream.

PLUM OR DAMSON DUMPLING

Plums and damsons were among the few English fruits to appear in fruit tarts and pies as early as the twelfth century. This dumpling is a real winter pudding – flavoursome, but filling!

8 oz/225 g flour
½ oz/15 g icing sugar
2 oz/50 g lard
4 fl oz/100 ml water
1¼ lb/575 g plums or damsons, whole
3 oz/75 g dark brown sugar
1½ oz/40 g butter

Serves 4

First make the hot water crust. Sieve the flour and icing sugar into a bowl. Melt the lard in the water and bring to the boil. Make a hollow in the middle of the flour and pour the boiling water and lard into it, stirring all the time to draw the flour into the paste. Knead gently with the hands until it forms a compact ball.

Flour a tea-cloth and roll out the paste thinly upon it. Pile the plums or damsons in the middle of the paste and sprinkle over 1½ oz/40 g of the brown sugar. Carefully draw up the edges of the paste and seal them together at the top with a little water. Tie the cloth around the dumpling to hold it in position.

Place the pudding in its cloth in the top of a steamer and steam briskly for 1½ hours. When the pudding is cooked, turn it carefully onto a warmed plate, trying not to break the crust. Melt the butter and pour it over the pudding, then sprinkle with the remaining sugar. Serve at once.

ICED GINGER CREAM

Ginger, like sugar, was regarded as a medicine in the Middle Ages. It was thought to 'quicken the remembraunce', to strengthen the teeth and to be an excellent remedy for toothache. Although it had lost its medicinal overtones by the eighteenth century, it still remained a very popular spice. Most large houses at this time had their own ice houses in the garden, so there would not have been any problem about chilling this dessert.

    5 fl oz/150 ml double cream
    1 oz/25 g stem ginger, thinly sliced
    1½ oz/40 g sugar
    2 oz/50 g toasted nibbed almonds
    2 tablespoons brandy
    1 egg white
    pinch of salt

Serves 4

Whisk the cream until it begins to hold its shape. Fold in the ginger, sugar, nuts (reserving a few for decoration) and the brandy. Whisk the egg white with the salt and fold into the cream mixture.

Spoon into individual dishes, sprinkle with the remaining nuts and freeze for 1 hour before serving.

'AN ORANGE PUDDING'

This tart is an excellent illustration of how twentieth-century gadgetry has reduced the cook's work. When Miss Smith wrote her recipes in 1727, her pestle and mortar would have been called into play to 'pound the orange rinds' and to 'beat the almonds very fine'. If you have ever tried performing this feat with a pestle and mortar you will know how very laborious it is!

pared rind and juice of 2 oranges
5 oz/150 g butter
4 oz/100 g granulated sugar
2½ oz/65 g nibbed almonds
3 eggs plus 2 egg yolks
6 oz/175 g sweet shortcrust pastry
several thin slices of orange

Serves 6

Put the rind of the oranges in a small pan with the orange juice, bring to the boil and simmer until the rinds are tender. Purée the juice and rinds in a food processor or liquidiser.

Beat the butter with an electric or rotary mixer until soft. Gradually add the sugar, then the almonds, eggs and orange purée.

Line an 8-inch/20-cm flan case with the pastry. Spoon in the orange mixture, decorate with the orange slices and bake in a moderately hot oven (190°C/375°F/Gas Mark 5) for 35 minutes. Serve hot.

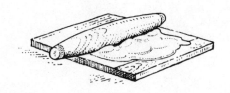

WHISKED CLARET PUFFS

Dr Johnson would undoubtedly have considered this recipe an excellent way of dealing with claret! As a drink, he thought it only fit for boys because it was so weak that 'a man would drown in it before it made him drunk.'

5 fl oz/150 ml single cream
5 fl oz/150 ml double cream
5 fl oz/150 ml claret
1½ oz/40 g castor sugar
1 oz/25 g toasted almonds
ratafias or Bosworth jumbles

Serves 6

Whisk together the creams and the claret and sweeten with the sugar. Pile into glasses and chill for several hours. Decorate with almonds and serve with ratafias or jumbles.

MACAROON TRIFLE

The medieval passion for almonds did not die with the Wars of the Roses, but as the centuries wore on the almonds tended to be cooked and used as sweetmeats and in biscuits rather than in savoury dishes.

In this recipe the almonds appear as macaroons and are combined with a typical eighteenth-century syllabub to make a trifle.

8 oz/225 g broken macaroons
4 tablespoons apricot jam
2 fl oz/50 ml sweet sherry
2 fl oz/50 ml brandy
8 fl oz/225 ml double cream
juice of 2 lemons
1 oz/25 g castor sugar
1 oz/25 g toasted nibbed or flaked almonds

Serves 6

Mix the macaroons with the apricot jam and put them in the bottom of a glass bowl. Mix the sherry and brandy and pour half the quantity over the macaroons and jam.

Whisk together the cream, lemon juice and sugar and the remains of the brandy and sherry. Pile this on top of the trifle and chill for several hours.

Before serving, decorate with almonds.

LEMON BOODLES FOOL

Lemon Boodles fool is a tart version of the famous orange Boodles fool which titillated the palates of the Victorian gentlemen who belonged to Boodles Club in St James's. The nineteenth century was the heyday of men's clubs (no women allowed!) and they vied with each other to obtain the services of famous French chefs, such as Ude or Alexis Soyer, the designer of the kitchens at the Reform Club.

    1 small sponge cake
    4 lemons
    2 oranges
    20 fl oz/600 ml double cream
    approximately 1 oz/25 g castor sugar

Serves 6

Break up the sponge and scatter it over the bottom of a 7-inch/18-cm soufflé dish.

Grate the rind from the fruit and squeeze out the juice. Lightly whip the cream and fold in the rind and juice. Sweeten to taste with sugar, and add more lemon juice if the mixture is not sufficiently tart.

Spoon the mixture over the sponge cake. (If you pour it, the sponge will float to the top!) Cover and chill for at least 6 hours, or overnight.

The juice will gradually sink through the cream into the sponge below, leaving a frothy cream on top.

Decorate with twists of lemon before serving.

HEDGEHOG TIPSY-CAKE

Throughout history dishes that look like live animals have been popular. Often these dishes were made from the actual animal: the peacocks and suckling pigs of the Middle Ages; the baked hares of the Victorian period served sitting up on their dishes with their ears cocked! Fortunately for the queasier stomachs of the twentieth century, this hedgehog only resembles a live hedgehog in its shape.

1 stale Victoria sponge or Madeira cake, approximately 9 in/
  23 cm in diameter and fairly thick
15 fl oz/450 ml sweet sherry or fruit wine
2 tablespoons apricot jam
1 tablespoon grated chocolate
4 large raisins
3 oz/75 g flaked almonds
10 fl oz/300 ml double cream
juice of 1 orange
juice of ½ lemon
approximately 2 tablespoons castor sugar
2 tablespoons red currant jelly

Serves 8

Cut the cake into a hedgehog shape and cut a well in the middle of its back, reserving the piece you take out. Put the hedgehog onto a serving dish and fill the well in its back with sherry or wine. Keep pouring the sherry or wine into the well and over the whole hedgehog until it is all absorbed. Replace the plug in its back.

Spread apricot jam all over the hedgehog and sprinkle with grated chocolate. Stick 2 raisins in its 'face' for eyes (with an almond flake over each) and 2 for a nose. Then stick the rest of the almonds into the cake, facing backwards to look like spikes.

Whisk the cream with the orange and lemon juice and sweeten to taste with the sugar; pile it round the hedgehog. Finally put a heap of red currant jelly in front of its nose as though it were eating it!

'MERINGLE PUDDING'

Apple pie has always been a firm favourite with the English. It was said of Lord Dudley, Queen Victoria's foreign secretary in the early 1850s, that he 'could not dine comfortably without his apple pie'. He was even heard to mutter, quite audibly, at a grand dinner held by Prince Esterhazy, 'God bless my soul – no apple pie . . . God bless my soul!'

Mr Williamson's recipe eschews the pastry lid in favour of meringue, but in all other essentials keeps within the tradition.

8 oz/225 g shortcrust or puff pastry
20 fl oz/600 ml water
3 oz/75 g sugar
3 lb/1.35 kg cooking apples, peeled, cored and cut in quarters
3 egg whites
7 oz/200 g icing sugar
1 teaspoon lemon juice
glacé cherries to decorate

Serves 8

Roll out the pastry and line an 8-inch/20-cm flan case; bake it blind.

Bring the water and sugar to the boil, add the apples and boil gently until they are soft but still in one piece. Remove them with a slotted spoon and pile them into the pastry case. Cool.

Beat the egg whites, sugar and lemon juice together until shiny and very stiff – this may take 3 or 4 minutes with an electric beater. Pile or pipe the meringue over the apples so that they are completely covered, and decorate with glacé cherries.

Cook for 30 minutes in a cool oven (150°C/300°F/Gas Mark 2) or until the meringue is set and lightly coloured. Serve either warm or cold.

'A PRETTY GRAPE JELLY'

Alexis Soyer suggests that 'for a ball supper' one should hang a bunch of grapes to set in a jelly mould. But however impressive the idea may sound, the problems of serving and eating a jellied bunch of grapes make one suspect that he had never actually tried it himself!

15 fl oz/450 ml water
5 fl oz/150 ml cherry brandy or cherry herring
1 oz/25 g dark brown sugar
4 fl oz/100 ml brandy
½ oz/15 g gelatine
12 oz/350 g grapes, peeled and seeded

Serves 6

Put the water, cherry brandy and sugar in a saucepan and boil briskly until reduced to 15 fl oz/450 ml. Put the gelatine in a bowl and gradually add the hot liquid, stirring all the time until the gelatine has melted.

Lay the grapes in the bottom of a fluted mould and pour in the jelly. Chill for several hours until quite firm. Turn out and serve, either as it is or with pouring cream.

COMPOTE OF PRUNES &
APRICOTS

*Although most of the old, country remedies have proved to be soundly
based, one does find some strange ideas lurking in the herbals and
garden books of the sixteenth and seventeenth centuries. For example, this is what John Gerard, Lord Burghley's gardener at
Theobalds, had to say on the subject of apricots: 'The fruit of the
abrecock, being taken after meate do corrupt and putrify in the
stomache; being eaten first, before meate, they descend easily and
cause other meates to pass down the sooner.'*

Fortunately, this particular theory has been disproved.

1½ lb/700 g mixed dried apricots and prunes
4 fl oz/100 ml sweet sherry
4 oz/100 g dark brown sugar
1 stick cinnamon
rind and juice of 2 oranges
20 fl oz/600 ml water

Serves 8

Soak the fruit overnight in a bowl of water. Drain and
discard the water.

Cut the orange rind into thin strips. Put the sherry,
sugar, cinnamon stick and orange rind in a saucepan with
the water and gradually bring to the boil. Add the fruit
and simmer gently for 15 minutes or until the fruit is
cooked. Remove the cinnamon stick, add the orange juice
and stir well.

Pour the fruit and juice into a serving dish. Serve either
warm or cold with cream or yoghurt.

CRYSTAL PALACE PUDDING

When the Great Exhibition was opened by Queen Victoria and Prince Albert at the Crystal Palace in 1851, the palace itself, built entirely of glass and steel, was the greatest marvel of all.

The Crystal Palace pudding is, of course, meant to represent the palace with its clear, jelly walls and exotic contents. Despite the lack of refrigerators for easy chilling, jellies had been enormously popular since the end of the eighteenth century. Indeed, so many were served at the Great Exhibition that isinglass (the normal setting agent made from fish gut or calves' feet) doubled in price and calf and buffalo skins had to be imported as the supply of fish gut and calves' feet ran out!

$\frac{1}{4}$ oz/10 g gelatine
3 fl oz/75 ml lime juice
7 fl oz/200 ml boiling water
2 egg yolks
$\frac{1}{2}$ oz/15 g castor sugar
5 fl oz/150 ml single cream
$\frac{1}{2}$ oz/15 g gelatine
15 fl oz/450 ml fresh fruit purée, preferably something fairly sharp such as raspberries, Victoria plums, red currants etc
$\frac{1}{2}$–1 oz/15–25 g pistachio nuts

Serves 6

Take two fluted jelly moulds of approximately 1-pint/600-ml capacity.

Make the jelly by softening $\frac{1}{4}$ oz/10 g gelatine in the lime juice, and then add the boiling water and stir until it is absolutely clear. Pour the jelly into one mould. Put the other mould inside and carefully fill it with weights until the liquid jelly just comes up to the top of the mould. Chill until set.

Remove the weights and pour a little hot water into the inner mould to free it from the jelly; lift out and replace the outer mould in the fridge.

Beat the egg yolks in a bowl and add the sugar and cream. Put the bowl over a pan of boiling water and heat gently, stirring continually until the mixture thickens slightly; it should just coat the back of the spoon. Cool.

Soften $\frac{1}{2}$ oz/15 g gelatine in a tablespoon of water. Add 4 tablespoons of the fruit purée and heat the mixture over boiling water until the gelatine has dissolved. Allow the gelatine mixture to cool slightly and then stir into the rest of the fruit purée. Fold the custard into the purée and allow the mixture to cool until cold but not set.

Meanwhile, decorate the inside of the mould with pistachio nuts pressed into the jelly in whatever pattern you fancy: flowers, windows to represent the Crystal Palace or simply a geometric design.

When it is ready, spoon the fruit mixture into the mould, smooth the top and chill until firmly set.

To turn out, dip the mould briefly into boiling water and turn out onto a serving dish. The jelly can be decorated even further with whipped cream or crystallised flowers around the base.

Baked Goods ~ breads, sweetmeats & biscuits

LARDY CAKE

The earliest cakes were no more than small lumps of bread dough left over from the weekly bake, to which were added a few dried fruits or spices.

To taste lardy cake at its best, it should be eaten warm, when the smell of the spices alone will make one's mouth water!

1 oz/25 g fresh yeast
$\frac{1}{2}$ teaspoon sugar
10 fl oz/300 ml warm water
$\frac{1}{2}$ teaspoon salt
1 lb/450 g plain flour
10 oz/375 g lard
$\frac{1}{4}$ teaspoon each ground nutmeg, allspice and cinnamon
3 oz/75 g dark brown sugar
1 oz/25 g mixed currants and sultanas

Cream the yeast with the sugar and water.

Sift the salt with the flour into a basin and make a plain dough by mixing the flour thoroughly with the sugar, water and yeast mixture. Knead the dough until it is smooth. Set it aside, covered, in a warm place until it has almost doubled in size. Knead gently a second time.

Roll the dough out into a rectangle $\frac{1}{2}$ in/1 cm thick and dot with one-third of the lard. Mix the spices with the sugar and divide into four. Sprinkle one portion over the dough. Fold into three as for flaky pastry, roll out, dot and sprinkle twice more, and then roll into a square.

Move the dough onto a baking sheet. Sprinkle the remaining portion of sugar and spices, mixed with the fruit, over the top.

Bake the cake for 20–30 minutes in a hot oven (210°C/ 425°F/ Gas Mark 7) until it is browned but not burnt. Remove onto a cooling rack and eat while still warm.

If it is not finished at the first sitting, the cake can be warmed through quite successfully.

MEDIEVAL GINGERBREAD

Gingerbread, which in medieval times was just that, gingered bread, is among the most venerable of English dishes. In the Middle Ages, knights engaging in feats of arms at a joust or tournament would present pieces of gingerbread to their ladies. These pieces of gingerbread would be formed in the shape of a shield, studded with cloves to resemble studs and painted with egg white to represent the knight's polished leather shield.

8 oz/225 g clear honey
¼ teaspoon ground black pepper
½ teaspoon ground cinnamon
1 teaspoon ground ginger
8 oz/225 g brown breadcrumbs
cloves
1 egg, separated

Warm the honey in a saucepan. Add the ground spices and stir well to mix. Add the breadcrumbs and again stir very well, making sure that the crumbs absorb all the honey. Cook gently for 2 minutes, but do not burn.

Turn the mixture onto a flat board and spread with a spatula or with your hands; it should be about ½ in/1 cm thick. Cut out shields, or whatever shapes you fancy. Decorate with the cloves and dot the top of each clove with egg yolk to 'gild' it.

Cook in a slow oven (150°C/300°F/Gas Mark 2) for 15 minutes to solidify the egg yolk. Cool.

When completely cold, paint the gingerbread with egg white and place in a dish to chill for at least 24 hours before serving.

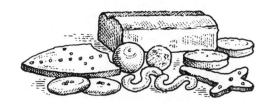

'GOOD BROWN BREAD'

Attempts were made to regulate the price and quality of bread as early as the thirteenth century. For example, the 'assize of bread' of 1266 states that punishments for selling 'bad bread' should include 'being drawn upon a hurdle through the great streets where most people be assembled and that be the most dirty, with the faulty loaf hanging about his neck.'

½ teaspoon dark brown sugar
½ tablespoon fresh yeast
10 fl oz/300 ml warm water (approximately blood heat –
    43°C/110°F)
1 lb/450 g wholemeal flour
1 teaspoon black treacle
pinch of salt

Mix the sugar and yeast and add half the water. Put the mixture in a warm place until it froths. This will take 10–20 minutes.

Put the flour and salt in a bowl. Mix the treacle with the remaining warm water. Make a well in the flour and pour in both liquid mixtures. Mix well by hand and knead for a couple of minutes.

Turn the dough into a greased 8-inch/20-cm loaf tin, cover with a cloth and leave in a warm place for approximately 30 minutes to rise until it has almost doubled its original size.

Bake for 10 minutes in a hot oven (200°C/400°F/Gas Mark 6), then reduce the temperature to 180°C/350°F/Gas Mark 4 and bake for a further 30–40 minutes or until the loaf sounds hollow when rapped with the knuckles.

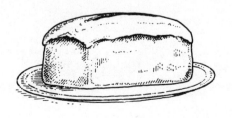

ALMOND BREAD

In Tudor times, Fynes Moryson wrote that 'the English husband-men eat barley and rye brown bread, preferring it as it abideth in the stomach; but citizens and gentlemen eat most pure white bread' – which presumably did not!

This almond bread, with its high proportion of expensive ground almonds and sugar must have been the perquisite only of the very wealthy – although its 'abiding' qualities might well have been greater than the average wheaten loaf!

4 oz/100 g ground almonds
2 oz/50 g wholemeal flour
1 teaspoon baking powder
2 oz/50 g granulated sugar
juice and rind of ½ lemon
1 oz/25 g butter
2 eggs, separated

Mix the almonds, flour, baking powder and sugar together in a bowl. Melt the butter and add it to the mixture along with the egg yolks. Beat well and then beat in the lemon rind and juice.

Whisk the egg whites lightly and stir into the mixture.

Pour into a small, 6-inch/15-cm, well-greased loaf tin and bake in a moderately hot oven (190°C/375°F/Gas Mark 5) for 25 minutes or until the loaf has risen slightly and is cooked – test with a skewer. Cool on a wire rack.

OATCAKES

Yorkshire oatcakes, made with yeast, salt and water mixed into the oatmeal, used to be 'thrown upon a bak stone', where the heat immediately 'puffed' them up. When cooked, they remained damp and limp and had to be hung on a clothes rail before the fire to dry.

Thanks to the invention of baking powder such drastic action is no longer necessary!

> 8 oz/225 g mixed oatmeal – fine, medium and coarse
> 4 oz/100 g plain flour
> ½ teaspoon salt
> 1 teaspoon baking powder
> 1½ oz/40 g butter
> 1½ oz/40 g lard

Put the mixed oatmeal in a basin and sift in the flour, salt and baking powder. Rub in the fats as for pastry, and mix to a stiff dough with cold water.

Turn the mixture onto a board sprinkled with oatmeal. Knead the dough lightly, roll it out and cut it into 3-inch/7.5-cm rounds. Place on a tray and bake in a moderate oven (180°C/350°F/Gas Mark 4) for 25 minutes.

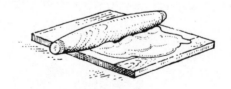

BOSWORTH JUMBLES

The story goes that the recipe for these little biscuits dropped from Richard III's pocket as he searched for a horse on Bosworth field. It would, no doubt, be unwise to enquire why he should have carried this recipe with him into battle, but the biscuits are excellent!

6 oz/175 g butter
1 lb/450 g castor sugar
1 egg
1 teaspoon powdered cinnamon
8 oz/225 g plain flour

Cream the butter with the sugar until pale and fluffy, then add the egg and beat again. Add the cinnamon to the flour and beat this into the mixture, which should be fairly stiff.

Knead the dough lightly and shape into small rolls approximately 3 in/7 cm in length. Form these either into 'S' shapes or into crossed swords and place on a greased baking tray. Bake in a warm oven (160°C/325°F/Gas Mark 3) for 25 minutes or until they begin to turn colour.

MRS BLENCOWE'S
GINGERBREAD

Mrs Blencowe's recipe appears at a halfway point in the develop-ment of gingerbread, from the medieval 'gingered-bread' to the ginger cakes and biscuits of the nineteenth and twentieth centuries. Grated breadcrumbs have given way to flour, and honey to treacle and sugar, but although the 'bread' is cooked no raising agent is used. The result is a very rich and filling cake-bread, not unlike a Yorkshire parkin.

> 1 lb/450 g plain flour
> ½ oz/15 g ground ginger
> a pinch each of cinnamon and nutmeg
> 4 oz/100 g dark brown sugar
> 1 oz/25 g candied peel
> 4 oz/100 g butter, softened
> 1 lb/450 g black treacle

Sift the flour and spices into the bowl of an electric mixer. Add the sugar and peel, then the softened butter and the treacle. Beat hard until the ingredients form a stiff paste.

Press this paste into a 10-inch/25-cm greased loaf tin. Bake in a moderate oven (180°C/350°F/Gas Mark 4) for 45 minutes. Remove and cool on a rack. Eat with butter.

CHOCOLATE JUMBALLS

When chocolate first appeared in England it was claimed that the cocoa nut had 'wonderful facility for quenching the thirst, allaying hectic heats and of nourishing and fattening the body . . .' We certainly would not disagree with the last point! The nib was usually pounded and boiled with milk, then thickened with eggs to make a hot chocolate drink very much enjoyed by eighteenth-century ladies.

In this recipe, cocoa powder is used to make little sweetmeats to be eaten after dinner.

4 oz/100 g ground almonds
6 oz/175 g castor sugar
$\frac{1}{2}$ oz/15 g cocoa powder
1 egg white
1 teaspoon lemon juice
1 teaspoon rosewater
a few dried apricots

In an electric mixer beat the almonds, sugar, cocoa powder, egg white, lemon juice and rosewater until they form a compact mass.

Cut the dried apricots into tiny pieces. Roll the mixture into about 48 small balls, and place them on a well-oiled baking tray. Press a piece of dried apricot into each.

Bake in a cool oven (130°C/250°F/Gas Mark $\frac{1}{2}$) for 15–20 minutes. The jumballs should still be slightly soft when they come out of the oven. Remove them carefully from the baking tray with a spatula. Cool on a wire rack.

PEPPER CAKES

Sweetmeats in medieval and Tudor times were always served after the meal. They consisted mainly of 'marchpane', or marzipan drops, and comfits – seeds and spices, such as caraway, coated in sugar. With the sweetmeats, guests would drink spiced wines – and be entertained by musicians and masqueraders.

This recipe really does use peppercorns . . .

    4 fl oz/100 ml medium sweet sherry
    2 fl oz/50 ml water
    1 tablespoon whole white peppercorns
    8–12 oz/225–350 g icing sugar

Put the sherry, water and peppercorns in a saucepan. Bring to the boil and simmer, uncovered, until the liquid is reduced to 4 fl oz/100 ml. Remove the peppercorns.

Gradually sift in the icing sugar, stirring all the time until the mixture forms a fairly stiff paste. Put into a forcing bag with a rose nozzle and pipe the mixture in small rosettes onto a lightly-greased baking tray.

Leave to dry, uncovered, for 3–4 days. Do not refrigerate. Turn over and leave for another 24 hours to dry out completely. Serve with coffee.

WIGS

Wigs were small white buns, 'taken with a glass of sack or Madeira' or dunked in a cup of breakfast chocolate. Maybe it was because the English were so enthralled by the deliciousness of their wigs and chocolate that La Rochefoucauld found them so taciturn at breakfast: 'Breakfast consists of tea and bread and butter in various forms. In the houses of the rich you have coffee, chocolate and so on. The morning papers are on the table and those who want to do so read them during breakfast so the conversation is not of a lively nature . . .'

6 oz/175 g flour
1 oz/25 g castor sugar
1 teaspoon baking powder
2 oz/50 g butter
5 fl oz/150 ml milk

Makes approximately 20 buns

Sift the flour, sugar and baking powder into a bowl and make a slight well in the middle. Heat the butter and milk together in a saucepan until the butter is melted and the milk just boiling. Pour the liquid into the well in the flour, stirring continually to draw in all the dry ingredients. Knead lightly to a smooth dough.

Drop large teaspoonfuls of the dough onto a greased baking sheet and cook in a moderate oven (180°C/ 350°F/Gas Mark 4) for 45 minutes.

The buns are excellent for breakfast or for tea.

RATAFIA BISCUITS

Little macaroons or ratafia biscuits were always popular; they often accompanied the creams and jellies enjoyed by ladies at ball suppers.

4 oz/100 g ground almonds
6 oz/175 g castor sugar
1 oz/25 g butter, melted
1 egg white
approximately 36 flaked almonds

Makes approximately 36 biscuits

Put the ground almonds, sugar, butter and egg white in an electric mixer and beat together until they form a compact mass. Roll the mixture into small balls, each the size of a walnut, and place them on a well-oiled baking sheet. Press one flaked almond into the top of each, thereby flattening the biscuit slightly.

Bake in a cool oven (130°C/250°F/Gas Mark ½) for 30 minutes. Remove carefully from the tray with a spatula and cool on a wire rack.

The biscuits will harden as they cool.

ROSQUILLONS

'To make rosquillons,' says the recipe, 'take fine Flower, the yolks of two Eggs, two ounces of butter melted and half a pint of thick Creame, work these together up into a stiff paste with fine flower, then rowle it out aboute the thicknesse of a Pye lid, then take march pane Paste and Rowle it out about the length and thickness of an arrow and wrap it up in the other Paste and cut them with a jaging Iron and make them in Knotts and sett them upon Pappers and bake them and so use them.'

These delicious eighteenth-century Danish pastries are best eaten about ten minutes after they come out of the oven, when they are still warm. They should not be kept for more than 24 hours; they will quickly lose their crispness and become leaden.

2 oz/50 g butter, melted
4 fl oz/100 ml double cream
2 egg yolks
6 oz/175 g flour
4 oz/100 g marzipan
½ oz/15 g castor sugar

Beat the butter, cream and egg yolks into the flour, and knead the mixture until it forms a smooth paste.

Roll the paste into a strip approximately 5 in/13 cm wide. Roll the marzipan into a long tube, approximately ½ in/1 cm in diameter, and place it down the middle of the paste. Cut diagonally into the paste, almost up to the marzipan, on either side at 1-inch/2·5-cm intervals. Plait the paste to make a knotted roll.

Carefully transfer the roll to a baking tray and bake in a moderately hot oven (190°C/375°F/Gas Mark 5) for 25 minutes or until the paste is cooked and lightly coloured. Sprinkle with sugar, slice and serve while still warm.

MRS MARSHALL'S GINGER SNAPS & GINGER NUTS

By the nineteenth century, medieval gingerbread had undergone many transformations, including one recipe which involved boiling breadcrumbs in claret and flavouring them with liquorice and aniseed! The Victorians enjoyed two types of gingerbread: the ginger cake made with flour and eggs, and ginger snaps or nuts – crisp little biscuits like these of Mrs Marshall's.

Ginger snaps
 4 oz/100 g butter
 2½ oz/65 g castor sugar
 3 fl oz/75 ml black treacle
 pinch ground mace
 ½ oz/15 g ground ginger
 ½ oz/15 g ground nutmeg
 rind of ½ lemon, finely chopped
 1 oz/25 g mixed peel, finely chopped
 1 oz/25 g blanched almonds, finely chopped
 1 egg
 5 oz/150 g plain flour, sifted
 mixed peel and flaked almonds to decorate

Melt together the butter, sugar and treacle. Cool, and then add the spices, lemon rind, mixed peel, chopped almonds and the egg. Mix well together, then add the flour and beat thoroughly. Set aside in a cool place for several hours, during which time the mixture will thicken and become manageable.

 Roll out on a lightly-floured board – the biscuits should be quite thin. Cut out the biscuits with a fancy cutter and decorate with flaked almonds and peel. Bake in a moderate oven (180°C/350°F/Gas Mark 4) for 15 minutes. Cool on a wire rack.

Ginger nuts

 4 oz/100 g plain flour, sifted
 1 oz/25 g ground ginger
 rind of 1 orange and 1 lemon, finely chopped
 1½ oz/40 g dark brown sugar
 1½ oz/40 g butter
 2 oz/50 g black treacle

Mix the flour with the ginger, orange and lemon rind and the sugar. Melt the butter with the treacle and then add the dry ingredients. Mix thoroughly until it forms a stiff paste, and leave to cool in the refrigerator.

Roll the mixture out thinly on a lightly-floured board and cut with fancy cutters. Bake on buttered greaseproof paper in a moderately hot oven (190°C/375°F/Gas Mark 5) for 12 minutes. Cool on a wire rack.

SEED BUNS

Caraway seeds have always been thought of as very 'medicinable';
their main virtues being the relief of indigestion and flatulence and
the sweetening of the breath. In the Middle Ages they were rolled in
crystallised sugar and carried on the person in decorated boxes. By
the eighteenth and nineteenth centuries they were usually baked into
small cakes or biscuits 'to be taken with a glass of wine'.

3 oz/75 g butter
1 egg
12 fl oz/350 ml warmed milk
1 fl oz/25 ml sweet sherry
2 oz/50 g castor sugar
10 oz/275 g flour
5 teaspoons baking powder
pinch each of salt and nutmeg
3–4 teaspoons caraway seeds, depending on taste

Makes approximately 20 buns

Melt the butter and allow to cool slightly. In a bowl, beat
the egg and mix in the milk, sherry and sugar, then add
the butter.

Sift the flour with the baking powder, spices and caraway seeds. Make a well in the dry ingredients, pour in the
liquid and stir quickly to mix.

Grease two bun or small cake tins and pour the mixture
into each hollow until two-thirds full. Bake in a hot oven
(210°C/425°F/Gas Mark 7) for 15–20 minutes or until the
buns are risen and lightly coloured.

Remove from the tins and cool on a wire rack.

MUFFINS

The muffin man, carrying his tray of fresh, hot muffins, was a familiar sight in the early morning streets of Victorian London. He always carried a bell, which he rang to summon the cook to the door to buy her mistress's breakfast for a penny a piece.

½ oz/15 g fresh yeast
1 level teaspoon castor sugar
10 fl oz/300 ml tepid water
1 lb/450 g plain white flour
1 level teaspoon salt

Makes approximately 12 muffins

Mix together the yeast, sugar and water. Mix the flour with the salt and add the yeast liquid. Stir well until a soft dough is formed.

Turn out onto a lightly-floured surface and knead for several minutes until smooth. Cover and leave in a warm place to rise to approximately double its size. Knead until firm and leave for another 5 minutes.

Roll out on a floured board to a thickness of ½ in/1 cm. Cover and leave for another 5 minutes. With a 4-inch/10-cm cutter, cut out rounds and place them on a floured baking tray. Leave to rise for a further 30 minutes.

Bake for 5 minutes at 230°C/450°F/Gas Mark 8, then turn and bake for a further 5 minutes.

Eat while still warm, with butter.

BATTENBERG

A Battenberg or 'chapel windows' cake is a development of the basic Victoria sponge – a firm favourite once Alfred Bird's baking powder started to appear regularly in the shops in the 1850s.

Before this, lightness in breads and cakes depended on yeast, eggs or such unlikely substitutes as snow. Mrs Rundell: '. . . two large handfuls of snow will supply the place of one egg. This is a useful piece of information especially as the snow often falls at the season when the eggs are dearest . . .'

Baking powder came into being because Mr Bird, a Victorian chemist, had a wife who was allergic to eggs and to yeast. Being a good chemist and a good husband, he set his mind to the problem and developed both custard powder and baking powder to ease her culinary problems!

4 oz/100 g butter
4 oz/100 g castor sugar
2 large eggs
4 oz/100 g flour
½ teaspoon baking powder
yellow and red colouring
raspberry jam
1 oz/25 g icing sugar
1 oz/25 g castor sugar
2 oz/50 g ground almonds
½ teaspoon lemon juice
½ egg white

Grease two 6-inch/15-cm loaf tins and line the bases with buttered greaseproof paper.

Beat the butter until soft, add the sugar and continue beating until light and fluffy. Beat in the eggs, and then the flour and baking powder mixed.

Divide the mixture in half. Add a few drops of yellow colouring to one half and quite a lot of red colouring to the other. The red mixture should be quite bright – the colour will fade in the cooking.

Cook the cakes in separate tins in a moderate oven (180°C/350°F/Gas Mark 4) for 25 minutes. Remove from the tins and cool on a rack.

To make the marzipan, sift the icing sugar into a bowl and mix in the sugar and ground almonds. Add the lemon juice and egg white and knead to a manageable dough, adding extra almonds and sugar if it is too soft.

Cut the cakes in half and trim to make four square-sided rectangular pieces. Using raspberry jam, stick them together to form a square with the pink sections and the yellow sections at opposite corners. Roll out the marzipan (using a little icing sugar to prevent it sticking) to a size that will cover the cake, and spread with jam. Place the cake on the marzipan and wrap it around, sealing the join at one corner with a little egg white. Trim the edges.

Cooks, Writers, Gourmets & Gourmands

Acton, Eliza
(1799–1859), Victorian lady poet who published her first recipe book, *Modern Cookery in all its Branches*, in 1845. She was the first cookery writer to separate the ingredients from the method in a recipe.

Beeton, Mrs Isabella
(1836–65), author of *Household Management*, first published in 1861. She contributed to her husband's magazine, *The Englishwoman's domestic magazine*, from which the material for her book was drawn.

Bennett, Arnold
(1867–1931), author and journalist.

Bird, Alfred
(1813–79), chemist and founder of a food manufacturing firm. His wife was allergic to eggs and to yeast and he invented custard and baking powder to act as substitutes.

Blencowe, Mrs Anne
(1656–?), wife of John Blencowe, Member of Parliament for Brackley, Northamptonshire. She kept her own collection of household simples, recipes, cures etc, which she turned into a book in 1694.

Boorde, Andrew
(1490–1549), a Carthusian monk who left the church at the Reformation to become a doctor and herbalist. He believed that health depended on diet and he published various works including *A dyetary of helthe* in 1542 and *A Breviary of Helthe*.

Brillat-Savarin, Anthelme
(1755–1826), famous French gastronome and author of *Physiologie du goût*, published in 1825.

Brummell, Beau
(1778–1840), dandy and man of fashion, favourite of the Prince Regent. He fell from favour and died in poverty.

Burton, Robert
(1577–1640), author of *Anatomy of Melancholy*, 1621.

Carême, Marie Antoine
(1784–1833), the most famous of all the Regency chefs; worked for the Tsar, the Duke of Wellington, the Rothschilds, the Prince Regent and Prince Talleyrand. Author of *La Cuisine française*.

Cobbett, William
(1763–1835), politician, journalist, reformer; a great believer in the idyll of a pre-industrial England.

Cooper, Joseph
head cook to Charles I. He published the *Art of Cookery refined & augmented* in 1654.

Cromwell, Joan/Elizabeth
wife of the Protector, Oliver Cromwell. Author of the *Court & Kitchin of Elizabeth, commonly called, Joan Cromwell*, published in 1664 by the Royalists.

Culpeper, Nicholas
(1616–54), great herbalist who wrote *The English Physician Enlarged or the Herbal* in 1653.

Dawson, Thomas
author of the *Good Housewife's Jewel*, published in 1585.

Defoe, Daniel
(1660–1731), author and journalist. Of interest to the food historian are a *Journal of the Plague year* and *A Tour of the whole Island of Great Britaine*.

Digby, Sir Kenelm
(1603–65), man of letters, greatly interested in science and one of the first members of the Royal Society; chancellor to Queen Henrietta Maria during the Interregnum. He wrote various scientific and philosophical treatises; best known for his posthumously published cookery book, *The Closet of the Eminently Learned Sir Kenelm Digby, knight, opened*, 1669.

East Indian friends
members of the East India Company who, through long residence in India, had acquired a taste for fiery dishes.

Elyot, Sir Thomas
(c. 1490–1546), author of *A Castel of Helthe*, 1538, a discourse on the maintenance of good health through diet.

Evelyn, John
(1620–1706), author, diarist, man of letters and a member of the Royal Society.

Farley, John
tavern keeper in London; published his recipes in *The London Art of Cookery & Housekeeper's complete Assistant* in 1783.

Fiennes, Celia
(1662–c. 1738), aristocratic, if eccentric, lady who made several expeditions all over England in the 1690s, travelling on horseback accompanied by one manservant.

Francatelli, Charles Elmé
(1805–76), cook to Queen Victoria; author of various cookery books in the high French style: *The Modern Cook*, 1845; *The Cook's Guide & Butler's Assistant*, 1861.

Gaskell, Mrs Elizabeth
(1810–65), novelist.

Gelleroy, William
cook to the Duchess of Argyll and author of *The London Cook or The Whole Art of Cookery made Easy and Familiar*, 1762.

Gerard, John
(1545–1612), gardener to Lord Burghley (Queen Elizabeth's treasurer) and author of *The Herball*, 1597.

Glasse, Hannah
(1708–70), published her cookery book, *The art of Cookery made plain and easy* in 1747; also known to have run a shop in Covent Garden and made clothes for the Royal Family.

Gronow, Captain
(1794–1865), soldier and man about town. In the early 1860s he published his memoirs, which detailed much of the gossip of early nineteenth-century society.

Gunn, Ben
a character in R. L. Stevenson's *Treasure Island.*

Harrison, William
(1534–93), topographer and author of *An historical description of the Ilande of Britaine*, 1577.

Johnson, Dr Samuel
(1709–84), famous lexicographer, critic and wit whose life was chronicled by James Boswell.

Kitchiner, Dr William
(1775–1827), an anatomist who was never allowed to practice because anatomy was not recognised as a medical science. He was famous as a gourmet who gave very recherché dinners and experimented with old or odd recipes. He published the *Cook's Oracle* in 1804.

Lamb, Patrick
(1647–1707), master cook and yeoman of the pastrie to Charles II, James II, William and Mary, Queen Anne; published *Royal Cookery or the Complete Court Cook* in 1710.

la Rochefoucauld, François, 6th Duc de
(1613–80), French wit and philosopher.

Markham, Gervase
(1598–1637), herbalist and author of *The English Huswife*, published in 1649.

Marshall, Mrs A. B.
author of *Mrs A. B. Marshall's Cookery Book*, c. 1880. Later editions specialised in more elaborate cuisine for the middle-class Victorian family. She also ran a cookery school.

May, Robert
(1588?–?), professional cook who worked for many noble families. *The Accomplisht Cook* was published in 1671.

Moryson, Fynes
(1566–1617), traveller and author of *An Itinerary*, 1617.

Moufet, Dr Thomas
(1595–1655), court physician who wrote *Health's Improvement or rules comprising the discovering the nature, method and manner of preparing all sorts of food used in this nation*, published in 1655.

Parkinson, John
(1567–1650), apothecary and gardener to James I; author of *Theatrum Botanicum*, 1640, for long the most comprehensive English herbal.

Paston, Margaret
(c. 1420–1484), member of the Norfolk gentry; wrote many letters to her husband who travelled extensively.

Pepys, Samuel
(1633–1703), diarist and clerk to the Navy Office. He is of particular interest to the food historian because of the details he gives of his domestic life.

Plat, Sir Hugh
(1552–1608), Elizabethan gentleman of scientific bent. He wrote various treatises on cookery and housewifery including *Delightes for Ladies*, published in 1609.

Raffald, Mrs Elizabeth
(1733–81), published *The Experienced English Housekeeper* in 1769. She was the mother of 15 daughters, kept a very successful food shop, ran two of the best inns in Manchester and also opened the first domestic agency.

Rundell, Mrs Maria
(1745–1829), author of *A new System of Domestic Cookery founded on principles of economy and adapted to the use of private families by a Lady*, first published anonymously in 1808.

Smith, Miss E.
author of a highly successful cookery book, *The Compleat Housewife*, first published in 1727.

Smith, Sydney
(1771–1845), parson, reformer, wit and diarist.

Soyer, Alexis
(1809–58), eccentric French chef who came to England in his early youth; designed and ran the kitchens at the Reform Club; ran soup kitchens for the poor during the famine in Ireland; worked with Florence Nightingale to improve conditions in the Crimea. Author of various cookery books including the *Poor Man's regenerator*, *A modern housewife*, and *Culinary Campaign in the Crimea*, 1857.

Tusser, Thomas
(1524–80), author of *Five Hundreth Pointes of Good Husbandrie*, published in 1573, a book of instruction for the yeoman farmer written in doggerel verse.

Ude, Louis Eustache
emigré from the French revolution. As a chef he worked for the Dukes of Sefton and York before taking over the kitchens of Crockford's Club. Author of *The French Cook*.

Verral, William
landlord of the White Hart Inn in Lewes in Sussex. Author of the *Cook's Paradise*, published in 1759.

Walpole, Horace
(1717–97), wit, diarist, letter writer, man about town.

Walton, Izaak
(1593–1683), author of the *The Compleat Angler, or the Contemplative Man's Recreation*, published in 1653.

Williamson, D.
published *Williamson's Cookery* in Edinburgh in 1870. He also ran a number of cookery classes.

Woodeforde, Parson
(1740–1803), country parson living in Norfolk. He kept a detailed diary which included many domestic details.

Wooster, Bertie
hero of P. G. Woodhouse's many *Jeeves* novels.

Index